Creating Tomo

D0343277

Also available from Continuum

Overschooled but Undereducated, John Abbott and Heather MacTaggart
The Coombes Approach, Susan Rowe and Susan Humphries

CREATING TOMORROW'S SCHOOLS TODAY

Education – Our Children – Their Futures

Richard Gerver

continuum

Dedication

To Lynne, Bethany and Andrew

xxx

Continuum International Publishing Group

The Tower Building
11 York Road
London SE1 7NX

15 East 26th Street
New York
NY 10010

www.continuumbooks.com

© Richard Gerver 2010

British Library Cataloguing-in-Publication Data
A catalogue record for this book is available from the British Library.

ISBN: 9781855393943 (paperback)

Designed and typeset by Ben Cracknell Studios
Printed and bound in Great Britain by Antony Rowe, Chippenham, Wiltshire

Contents

Acknowledgements

With love and thanks to my family and the people who helped me find my future.

Heartfelt thanks to all of those people who have encouraged and believed in me. To those who have guided me, to the children I have taught and who have taught me. To the many experts who have helped me learn about the craft that is teaching and the complexity of child development.

Particular thanks must go to Sir Ken Robinson, my mentor and inspiration; to Brendan Barns and his team at Speakers for Business; to James Hilton and Anne Riley, friends and former colleagues, who gave me the freedom to develop my early philosophy as a teacher.

Thanks also to all those at Continuum.

To Les Seymour for the photography and, more importantly, for his wisdom.

Finally, special recognition must go to the extraordinary children, staff, governors and parents at Grange Primary School, Long Eaton, who really created this book through their actions, creativity and commitment.

FOREWORD

Civilization, as H. G. Wells memorably said, is a race between education and catastrophe. If education is to win, we need urgently to pick up the pace of change in our schools. Most education systems around the world are being reformed. But reform is not enough. The truth is that we need a complete transformation in the principles and processes of public education. Educational transformation is what my own work has been about and it's what this book by Richard Gerver is about.

As a species and as a planet we are facing challenges that have no precedent in human history. They come in part from rapid population growth and the massive strains that our apparently insatiable appetites are putting on the world's natural resources. They come too from the unpredictable interplay with human cultures of accelerating innovations in science and technology. Many of these challenges are the direct result of the global convulsions of the Industrial Revolution, which are still reverberating around the earth. Our generation and the ones we're educating have to deal with these challenges, right now. The problem is that the dominant systems of education through which we're trying to do this are rooted in the values and methods of industrialism that created many of these challenges in the first place. Making these systems more efficient simply won't do. In the proper sense of the word, we need a new paradigm for education.

Industrial systems of education are essentially impersonal. They emphasize conformity in the curriculum and in teaching methods and standardization in assessment. And, too often, national systems of accountability treat students as raw materials and statistics as outcomes. A high degree of wastage is taken for granted. I know I'm simplifying here, but not much. You can get some idea of how wasteful these systems are by looking at the high rates of drop out and truancy among students and of turnover among teachers, especially from secondary schools, and at the precipitous rise in prescription drug use to keep students of all ages with the programme.

What these impersonal systems overlook is that education is always, essentially and inevitably, personal. I can't imagine there's a child anywhere who jumps out of bed in the morning wondering what he or she can do to raise the school district's reading scores. Students learn best if they're engaged, interested and motivated personally and, if they're not, they tune out and turn off. This was always true. It's even more important to understand this now. Young people are living in the most connected, information-driven period in human history. Their facility with technology and the appetite for networking show how eager they are to learn if the conditions are right. Creating these conditions means customizing education to each school, to each community of students, teachers, staff and parents, here and now. Thinking creatively about how to personalize and customize education is what this book is really about.

These days, education has four main roles. The first is *individual*. All children are born with immense, natural powers of imagination and curiosity. These come as standard in human beings. In addition to what they have in common, all children have their own particular aptitudes, dispositions and potential passions. One purpose of education has to be to help realize, in both senses of the word, the unique abilities of every student. The second role is *cultural*. Education should help our children understand the achievements and traditions of their own, and other communities, in an ethos of empathy and tolerance. The third is *economic*: to enable all students to achieve financial independence and contribute to wealth creation in ways that are ethical and sustainable. And the fourth is *social*. Effective schools sit at the heart of strong communities. Through outreach programmes, work with adults and partnerships with parents and families, schools must foster the spirit and practice of community life and responsibilities.

As you're about to find out, Richard Gerver is an exceptional educator whose work in schools shows that the value of personalizing and customizing education is not just a theory. His book shows that this is the best, and I believe the only, practical way to realize the talents of all our students and to help them engage in the real challenges they face. The book is in two parts. In Section 1, he sets out his view of the wider forces that are shaping education in these opening years of the twenty-first century. Against this background, in Section 2 he describes exactly how he and his staff transformed one failing school in England and saw it evolve in a few short years from neglect and despair to local success and international acclaim.

Informing all that Richard Gerver says and does is a deep, optimistic belief in the great qualities that this generation of young people brings with them to school. There's no question for me that this optimism for human possibility is a crucial factor in his outstanding success as a classroom teacher and as a school principal. His transformative work with the Grange School is also a compelling example of how the principles of personalizing and customizing education play out in practice, to the huge benefit of the children, the teachers, the parents and the wider community of the school. It is these principles that count.

Each school is different and every child is unique. Consequently, there isn't a single model of this new paradigm of education that will work everywhere. That's the whole point of this book. The task for educators is to apply these principles creatively with their own communities, to find what works best in their own here and now. It's the only approach to education that really works, and the only one that ever has. In this passionate, first-hand account of one teacher's and one school's journey, Richard Gerver shows both why and how this is true.

Sir Ken Robinson
October 2009

Grange Primary School transformed its approach to learning

PREFACE

The moral imperative

Our education begins from the moment of our conception and will shape the people we become, the lives we will lead and the impact we will have on others. It is surely the single most important part of human development. Whether we like it or not, consciously or subconsciously, we are learning; experiencing, processing and growing for as long as we draw breath.

Formal education, that is to say our schooling, provides the most potent part of our structured experience and therefore there is a moral imperative, an absolute, that those of us who have responsibility for it, as teachers and as parents, must keep at the forefront of our minds and at the heart of our thinking.

A sausage sandwich, or as we call it in my part of the world, a sausage cob, recently provided me with one of those moments, a moment of clarity and of deep thought. I was on my way to Aberdeen to give a speech on leadership to a number of small and medium-sized businesses. My journey began at my local airport, where, at 5.45 in the morning, my needs were simple. I wanted a sausage cob! So, with great purpose and the clarity of action that only hunger can bring on, I headed for the café. My eyes lit up as the counter came into view, behind which was a pyramid of carefully stacked, crisp, glistening sausages, next to a pile of fresh baked, crunchy white rolls . . . If there is such a thing as food heaven, then I had surely found it! As I reached the front of the queue, salivating at the thought of my breakfast treat,

I was met by Billy, a young man to do any former teacher proud. Billy was about 19 or 20 years old and he had already made it to the position of Senior Front of House Supervisor, I know because it said so on his badge. Billy was good at his job. He was not only a supervisor but he was a supervisor with five gold stars for customer service. Billy smiled and asked me what I would like. Without drawing breath, I requested my long desired meaty treat. It was at this moment that my culinary experience began to turn sour. Billy sucked air in through his teeth in that way that young people can, signalling that my request may not be as straightforward as I had assumed. Sadly, I was right. 'I am sorry, sir', he said with a highly trained, professional smile, 'We don't serve sausage cobs here.' Slightly confused, I looked at him and then over his left shoulder, at the sausage mountain under the heater light. After some further discussion, Billy kindly agreed to go into the kitchen and ask the catering manager if he may be able to sell me a sausage sandwich. The problem apparently being that the cash register only accepted full English breakfasts or bacon rolls. After a few minutes Billy returned with an air of positivity and told me that he thought he was able to sort out my 'problem'. He would not be able to sell me a sausage sandwich, but would be able to sell me a sausage and some bread!

Billy was genuinely a nice person, helpful and well trained. He had learned his job and was implementing it perfectly. He knew the rules and stuck to them. He demonstrated commitment to his job and clearly wanted to do well. He was a great product of our 'system'. However he couldn't cope with change, or a diversion from the norm; it threw him. In many ways, Billy is the perfect example of a young person educated in the current school system. He was technically efficient yet lacked the essential skills he would need to truly flourish in the world he now inhabits and the one he will continue to mature into. My first thought as I stood there in the queue by the cash register with a sausage on a plate in my right hand and a bread roll on a plate in my left was, 'Oh Billy, what have I done to you?'

We have become very good over the last hundred years or so at teaching our children. We have developed remarkably efficient systems for mass education that have brought learning and opportunity to 'the people'. Indeed we can look back proudly at a system that helped to fire the industrial age. We have, however, become wedded to our own success as a society and become complacent – to an extent, falling into the classic trap that lies in wait for anything successful, which is to enjoy the benefits and let the system take care of itself. As a result our system for mass education has remained largely unchanged. Experts have come and gone, theories and thinking have evolved and been trialled but little at the heart of the system has really been transformed. As a result we find ourselves in challenging, frustrating times in which many education professionals feel deeply the need for system transformation, as do many parents and prospective parents. Business leaders are crying out for young people to develop skills that are not honed by the current system, communities despair at the disconnected attitudes of many of their young and, in general, there appears to be confusion about what can be done. We are entering one of the most important phases of our global history, with challenges not just to the fabric of our societies but to our very existence as a species and to the planet on which we live. There are great thinkers and pragmatists around the world who agree that our system of education is not only partly to blame for the problem but also has, optimistically, the potential to play a major role in a successful future.

One of the most significant problems we face is that as a society, as teachers and as parents, we have felt a growing lack of empowerment that has left us at times despairing, wondering what we can do, where to begin, how to make the changes that are so necessary. Many look to governments, to experts, to academics and strategists to provide us with the answers, the rules for a new system that will set things right. Young people themselves are journeying through the education system feeling that same lack of empowerment, lacking a sense of relevance or purpose and together we all stand confused.

At the beginning of 2002 I was privileged enough to be given the passport to the greatest journey of my professional life. I was appointed the headteacher of Grange Primary School on the borders of Nottingham and Derby, two cities in the Midlands. As a parent and teacher I felt the same frustrations that many of us do and was given the opportunity to explore and develop my thinking by sharing it with the community around the school. By harnessing their views, skills, knowledge and commitment, together we were able to evolve a new approach for schooling our children that met many of the challenges the wider system faces. In this book I want to share some of that thinking and how Grange turned much of it into practice and, by doing so, created a vibrant and dynamic learning community that has captured the imagination of people around the world. Before I left Grange at the end of 2007 we had played host to visitors from over 50 nations including the United States, Russia, Australia and Iran, all looking to find models that could help them transform their schools.

When I became a teacher I joined the profession with a powerful sense of purpose, a moral imperative. I wanted to prepare the children in my care for their futures and to do so in a dynamic, exciting and rewarding way. I know when I talk to colleagues that it is a purpose that is widely shared. It is this purpose that has always driven me and one which I took into the job at Grange. This book is my way of expanding on that vision, that passion; explaining where it comes from and ultimately what it can look like when it is translated into practice.

To that end, the book has two sections: Section 1 explores my vision for education and the critical questions we must begin to answer. Section 2 tells the Grange story and sets out some of the approaches and systems we developed to transform Grange into the magical place it became for its children, its staff and its community.

SECTION 1

The challenge

CHAPTER 1

Education and the changing world

The imperative for change

'Tomorrow belongs to the people who prepare for it.'

African proverb

Could you make a list of the things that exist now that didn't 20 or 30 years ago when we were kids? It would be long and varied. That list could include not just technology, but television programmes, music, books, world orders, cultural shifts, working patterns. If we expanded that list back further, to our parents' and grandparents' generations, the lists would be almost infinite. The world is shifting second by second, even 'nano-second by nano-second'. There's a relatively new term, and I've started my list already.

In the time it has taken to write this sentence new discoveries and inventions have now begun to change the world in which we live. How many of us could have predicted the internet 30 years ago and the effect it would have on our lives? Who foresaw that the computing power in a mobile phone would be greater than that used to manage the *Apollo* space missions?

I recently discovered a quote that underlines the pace of change and the lack of ability we have to calibrate it. In 1949 a headline article was published in an American magazine called *Popular Mechanics* that proclaimed, with a degree of drama, that future computers might weigh less than 1½ tons.

From the first mass education systems of Victorian times up to today the system and the thinking behind the system have changed little, so in many ways schooling is becoming less and less relevant.

Education and the notion of mass education must surely be to prepare our children for successful lives as adult citizens. As a parent, I want my children to live happy, fruitful lives, making positive contributions to the world around them. I expect their schooling to prepare them for the challenges of the future and to help them develop the skills and behaviours that will see them flourish in the middle of the twenty-first century and beyond.

In order for schools to successfully meet these challenges, they need to have clarity about their role and about the patterns of future needs. This, of course, becomes scary territory. We can no better predict the future now than we could 50 years ago, as the article from *Popular Mechanics* magazine demonstrates. The world that our children will inhabit as adults is as far, if not further, removed from the one we live in as the one that we live in is from the world of our parents.

Developing essential IT skills

How on earth do we prepare children for a world that does not yet exist? Some argue, and have done for generations, that you stick to certainties. That you continue to improve the system as it is and as it was. We live in a world where we constantly hark back to our past to find solace and stability. The good old days will always be that, no matter when you were born or when the old days were. There is much in our system of learning that is vital to ensure the success of the journey, but seeing where it now fits, and with what, is the difficulty.

We do know something of the future and the changing shape of our lives. Crucially, much is centred on work and working patterns. For example, the financial landscape of our world has changed and is changing further. That has never been clearer than the events that began to unfold towards the end of 2008 when the global economic crisis began to have a profound impact on us all. The problems will leave a profound legacy on the world of work. For example, according to the *Annual Business Inquiry* report 2006, the percentage of people employed in the Financial and Related Business Services sector (FRBS), was 21.2 per cent of the total workforce in the UK. In London that figure was 33.5 per cent. In New York, the figure was 25 per cent of the workforce. Some commentators have predicted that by the end of 2009 job losses in the FRBS sector could reach as high as 20 per cent of employment globally. What will that do to the traditional notion of job patterns and security?

The continent of Asia, which has become the world's manufacturing base, will hold the key to much of the world's future employment patterns. China has recently redesigned its educational system, developing a new 'national curriculum' created to fan the flames of their industrial growth, in order to create employees who are focused and productive and who possess high levels of technical efficiency. It has a clarity and focus similar to that which led to the development of our mass education systems of the late nineteenth century.

Before then most formal education in the UK was linked to the church. Schooling was limited and mostly accessed in the private sector by the wealthy. That changed with the Forster Elementary Education Act in 1870 which led to the provision of schools for the vast majority of children between the ages of 5 and 10 who were required by law to attend school. The act of 1880 insisted on compulsory education and also required that any child employed under the age of 13 had to have a certificate to show that they had reached the educational standard. Subsequent acts, leading to the Fisher Act of 1918, made education for all compulsory to the age of 14. As the system evolved through the first half of the twentieth century it was focused on providing education to children in order to prepare them to fill new roles in the growing workforce, which saw a move from an agricultural-focused to an industrial-driven economy. By 1944 and the Butler Education Act, a system was developing that forms the basis for the system that most of us experienced as children. It defined the split between primary and secondary education and, significantly, the tripartite system, which developed the concept of grammar schools for the academically gifted and technical or secondary moderns for those who did not pass the selection tests.

From the outset the 1944 act caused controversy, with accusations of elitism on the one hand, while others argued that it allowed young people from any economic background the chance to enjoy a richly academic education, a privilege that had up until then been available only to the wealthy. In many ways the 1944 act has been the source of many of the arguments that still rage today and have hampered the genuine, objective development of our system. It is an area I will return to later in the book but it is important to recognize that compartment-alizing education and children into two camps may have benefited our national development during the Industrial Revolution and the period of our industrial dominance, as indeed it appears to be doing in China today. The education system born out of the Victorian age and the Butler Act was highly focused on the needs of the day, providing two distinct bands of future employees – white and blue collar workers – to staff our business and professional needs on the one hand and the industrial growth on the other. It also ensured that our system continued to cele-brate the British tradition of academia and research first established in the twelfth century with the rise of Oxford and Cambridge universities. For centuries education has evolved little but has, to an extent, mirrored society's needs. For many generations, and particularly since the post-war period, many have argued that education has been too academically focused, too narrow and too slow to react to the changes of the world its serves . . . and it is at this point we need to begin: with a view of the current and of the future worlds beyond school.

When children starting school now reach retirement age they will have worked in 18–25 different organizations or companies, compared to the four or five companies worked in by those retiring now. The reason for this is that companies will no longer be looking for committed people to train and manage for life, growing with a business through thick and thin, good times and bad. They will be looking to secure more and more people on short-term contracts, working to develop key areas of their development planning and then moving on as a company's plans and needs change. It is also interesting to flag up that the number of 2008 university graduates still looking for 'graduate-level' employment by the start of 2009 was approximately 30 per cent and that 'blue chip' companies are increasingly saying that a first-class degree is no longer a major criterion for employment selection.

This information helps us understand the nature of the challenge.

The world of our children will be even more uncertain than our own. The rapid development of globalization and communication means that the world will become more and more fragmented, depersonalized and decentralized. This may fill us with dread. Many of us may despair and desperately claw back to the 'good old days' in the hope that we can reverse these trends. The reality is that this will not happen and, in many ways, the reason the future looks so stark is because it is a world that we were not prepared for, a world that we would not feel comfortable in. It is not necessarily worse but it is very different and that is unsettling. The imperative is that it is a world in which our children will feel comfortable and will be prepared to lead their lives. It must be a world that they feel they have ownership of, a world that they are empowered to thrive in.

It is fascinating to see more and more people now raising their heads above the parapet and beginning to realize the challenges of tomorrow. In 2006 a teacher of technology from Arapahoe High School in Denver, USA set out to produce a slide presentation for the staff to instigate debate about the world our children would be living in as adults. His name was Karl Fisch and the presentation became *Shift Happens* which had been viewed on video-hosting sites such as YouTube over 5 million times before the end of 2007. This alone gives us a glimpse into the present, let alone the future: a world where thoughts and ideas can be shared across the world in seconds; ideas that can, within hours, become major international topics for debate.

So what kind of people will our children need to be? They will need, above all else, huge levels of self-confidence, they will need to be adaptable, utilize their natural creativity and understand their own strengths and weaknesses. They will need to be increasingly self-aware emotionally and intellectually and be capable of building relationships quickly, effectively and often 'virtually'. There are many who say that a spirit of entrepreneurship will be vital in our young, both for their own success and our economy's future stability. As I explore these skills and competencies, I find myself lacking in so many. I wonder, for example, how many of us are confident enough to share with others what our strengths are and whether we have a complete understanding of how to deploy them in a variety of contexts? I also wonder how many of us are confident of sharing what we are not very good at and, perhaps more challengingly, know how to deploy those weaknesses to best effect, rather than simply hiding behind them?

The key question, then, is: does our system explicitly seek to develop these 'soft skills' in its current state? Is it doing what it is designed for, preparing our children for the challenges of their future?

I recently spent some time in China, in Shanghai and in an industrial town called Hefei about two hours' flying time from Shanghai, with its technology, stunning architecture and relentless drive towards the future. While I do not see the Chinese system as a model of the future for us, it does help us explain the past and should help us understand our next steps. As I have already mentioned, the education system in China is designed and run with unbelievable efficiency: class sizes of 60, children attending school up to 6½ days a week, children of secondary-school age working on set homework for up to 5 hours every night. The curriculum is nationally prescribed with every child in every school working from the same page in the same textbook every day. Lessons are like lectures: young people are given huge amounts of information to process hour after hour, with breaks for formal mass exercise. Interestingly, English is a core subject. By the age of 12, most children can speak the language fluently. They also all give themselves English names; why? Because they know that speaking English will continue to give them a competitive advantage in their future. The system is awe-inspiring in many ways but, in others, terrifying. It does what it says on the tin: prepares its children to be able to exist with great efficiency in the industrial maelstrom that is China today. However the children are not explicitly developed to think for themselves and to question or create to any great extent. In many ways that is not the focus of the system because it is not what is needed for the majority at the moment in order for the nation to thrive. My experience helped me understand a little of our own past and why, for generations, it had worked. However, sitting in those classrooms, I could feel the narrow nature of the learning and particularly of the students' personal development. There appeared to be no vision for the development of the individual, helping them discover what made them unique and then nurturing those personal qualities.

I found myself returning from China with a mixture of emotions and a number of questions based on my experience. China has developed an education system that is at the core of its national vision. It has a culture steeped in the notion of one nation, one people, working together for one aim. To see and feel this was a powerful and, at times, profound experience and one which made sense of the education system they are developing. It left me asking: what is our national vision and how does it drive our education system? I'm not sure we have a vision, and as a result, it doesn't drive our educational system. Maybe therein lies a larger challenge. We have over the last 30 years developed short-term policy for short-term impact. Schools are seen as the vehicle to allay public fear across almost all areas of social ill: crime, racism, abuse, financial mismanagement, ecological crisis. The system has identified worthy and much needed areas for development and created policy which is expected to fit on top of or around the core philosophy which is still grounded in the traditional models of the pre-war period. In the last ten years, for example, we have had policies developed around the concepts of creativity, enjoyment, child safety and personalization, many of which schools have found difficult to implement with any real impact or longevity. The reason, I fear, is that tinkering around the edges with the things that need to be at the heart will never work and that is why we must look to the future with a clarity and confidence and redefine the purpose of schooling. Our children are not going to be entering a world where they will find jobs neatly packaged in to those two easy categories of white collar or blue collar. Neither will they find a world which will need simply academically good students or the rest. It was, ironically, in China that one experience reframed my purpose as an educator and perhaps the vision for our future and it based on an encounter I had towards the end of my trip to a secondary school in Hefei.

On the whole teachers would enter classrooms that resembled banked lecture halls; children would bow in reverence and thank the teachers for sharing their wisdom and knowledge, listen without interruption or question and then repeat the bowing ritual. Towards the end of my visit, I was sitting in a classroom where the kids were waiting with an expectancy I had not felt before; there was an air of excitement. In hobbled a wizened, old teacher, 70 if he was a day. The students fell respectfully quiet, the old guy shuffled slowly to the front of the room and bowed to his pupils and said, 'Dear students, thank you for attending my lesson today. I hope that some of what I am about to share will be of interest and importance.' He then proceeded to deliver what was, by Chinese standards, a highly interactive and dynamic session at the end of which he again bowed to his students and thanked them for their involvement and interest. Slowly he shuffled to the door and thanked them all individually as they left. Slightly taken aback by the nature of this session and the enlightened and, at times, moving experience, I asked this teacher for the reasons behind his approach. His explanation will stick with me forever!

> Every day, I stand in front of these young people, their faces full of expectation and hope, their energy radiating across the stale air of this room, and as I look across at them, I think to myself, somewhere in this room could be the person who finds the cure for cancer, the solution to world peace. Could be the person who

writes the next great symphony that moves mankind. There could be a future leader, doctor, nurse, teacher, Olympic champion. I don't know, but what I do know is that they are out there and it is my job to identify and nurture that talent, not just for their own benefit but for the possible benefit of others. Is there any greater responsibility or opportunity than that? I am blessed, that is why I thank them.

The words of this old man sum up for me why it is wrong for us to continue to pursue a model of education that primarily looks to create people to fit jobs. It was the efficient model at one time in our history and is the efficient model in China now. It was never, and never will be, perfect. It leaves too many people with too many valuable and fascinating skills and interests outside of a category and, therefore, unsure of who they are or what role they can play. In the present and in the future, where life is developing so fast and so unpredictably, the one thing we know is that we need to develop our uniqueness and our individual capacities. We need to leave school equipped to deal with a world that will still need academics, professionals, technicians and manual workers but that will also need people who will be able to invent the new jobs and ways of working that simply do not yet exist. For that reason we need to create a system that creates people who can make the jobs fit them.

CHAPTER 2

Harnessing the power of our children

Do we realize their potential?

Why is it that every generation mourns the passing of the last and fears the birth of the next? Why do we live in a world obsessed with demonizing our children? Our children are the same human beings we are, with the same capacity for good or bad; they are not born malevolent or seeking to destroy. Who they are and what they will become has been, and always will be, dependent on the environment that surrounds them and the legacy they inherit.

Author

'The children of today are thick, disruptive and out of control. I blame those computer games and the television. In my day . . . '

It's a common refrain heard all over the world in every supermarket, coffee shop and on street corners. Depending on who you ask, we blame parents, schools, the government, even 'e' numbers. The interesting thing is that every generation believes that the new kids on the block is the generation that will destroy humanity. Wasn't pop music supposed to be the spawn of the devil?

Perversely, the youth cultures of today are creating the problems of our new generations, but not for the reasons we feel comfortable believing. New generation after new generation has felt alienated by society and, therefore, to an extent, rebelled against it. It is true to say that our young are, in small numbers, more aggressive and less respectful of authority. There is, without doubt, a significant issue with gang cultures and violence, drugs, underage sex and alcohol abuse. Two recent reports – one for The National Children's Bureau in 2009 and one for The Equality Authority in Ireland in 2006 – reach the same conclusions, with one of the constant factors being that there is a feeling of a growing alienation from society and a desire to belong to something with status and stability. This is not a new discovery: *Delinquent Boys* by Albert K. Cohen, the famous American criminologist, which was published in 1955 highlights the reasons for youth crime and delinquency as being related to the factors of social exclusion, including low self-esteem and status, low academic achievement and social acceptance. Little has changed and, although there has been much talk about using education to help overcome these issues, it has yet to really be translated into any meaningful practice.

Clearly this is a massive issue which cannot be covered here but in the context of this book it is important to ask how we, as educators, ensure that our children experience an education system which develops their self-esteem and awareness, their aspirations and values, and their confidence as individuals to see the positive role they play as they emerge into society. In many ways our current system is brilliant at highlighting for children what they can't do but isn't very good at highlighting what they can. One of the gravest problems we face is that, through some elements of the media, all of our children have been tarnished by the stories of youth crime and delinquency which creates an even greater sense of social exclusion and fear. Carey Oppenheim, a co-director at the Institute for Public Policy Research said in 2007 that:

> The problem with 'kids these days' is the way adults are treating them. Britain is in danger of becoming a nation fearful of its young people: a nation of paedophobics. We need policy which reminds adults – parents and non-parents alike – that it is their responsibility to set norms of behaviour and to maintain them through positive and authoritative interaction with young people.

> *('Asbo Culture: Making Kids Criminal', Institute for Public Policy*
> *press release, 10 December 2007)*

Today's 'delinquents' are better equipped than any previous incarnations to face the challenges that surround us all. They are more aware of the world around them. Indeed according to Marc Prensky, an American digital media expert and educator, the technological revolution has changed the physiology of their brains. In his report 'Digital Natives, Digital Immigrants', published in 2001, Prensky argues that the complexity of the technology and information that surround our children has had a profound effect on the way their brains evolve, meaning that they are able to process high volumes of information at incredible speed but they are losing the ability to concentrate on one thing for a sustained period of time. Sadly, however, we are not helping them to make sense of this complex world overflowing with knowledge, opinion, choice and temptation. We are therefore adding to the generations of increasingly confused and alienated young people who are struggling to understand their emerging skills and knowledge. They believe that our world is irrelevant to them and that we are negative towards, almost scared of, their cultures and understanding. This may explain the exponential growth of a different form of gang culture. Is the growing involvement in virtual worlds and social networks not partly a symptom of a need to belong to something too?

While we are aware of the power and value of the interests, experiences and media that our children are exposed to, we are doing little to exploit them positively. As a system education is seen as the way to maintain traditional values, to lead the fight against the evolution and change of our societies. By clinging to those traditional learning routes and approaches, we will somehow be able to stem the flow of change and technology, to be able to regain control of a world that in many ways has become alien to us, and that is partly why we feel so unsettled, so threatened. 20 years ago parents had to ask their children to show them how to set the video recorder; today my children are teaching me how to develop an avatar presence on Second Life.

My daughter is an average teenager. She is interested in a huge variety of things and has a natural ability to understand and utilize new technologies in ways I marvel at. She, like most children, thrives best in her natural habitat, her bedroom. After tea she will retreat to her space. She puts on her TV and fires up her PC. She will be watching avidly the latest episode of her favourite gritty children's drama on the BBC. While absorbing what can at times be quite complex issues raised by the programme, she is playing her game of choice on her PC, which at present is a hospital-management simulation game. The object is to build, manage and develop hospitals to their full potential, dealing with hiring and firing, research, staff training, building plans, disease eradication, budgeting, etc. In effect, she is running the National Health Service from her bedroom, while watching the TV drama. She is good at it too, very good. She is currently managing a super hospital and has a surplus budget of near on £250 million. Not satisfied with running the Health Service and absorbing the pros and cons of life for a child in care being played out on the TV, she is also having a video MSN conversation with her grandma who lives in Spain. Oh, and she is also listening to the latest album released by some girl band with attitude which she has downloaded from a friend's iPod, mixed with software from the net and reconfigured to her own tastes. Finally, she is having a text-message conversation with a friend from school about their homework. The following day, she goes into school, sits at her desk working out of a textbook, spending an hour dissecting it. Are we really feeding our children's remarkable brain power and understanding of the world?

The real tragedy is that we are underestimating the potential of our young and of what they know and do. They are so much more independent as learners. They know innately how to find out new things without being told, they deploy new technologies without having to be shown. In fact they are discovering applications for devices that the experts themselves had not thought of. Ten years ago in our primary school, we needed to show children how to turn on a computer and help them to control a mouse. Today children starting in our nursery school system are navigating themselves through to the NickJr ® website and researching their favourite programmes as soon as they walk through the door. Our children have created a new language and means of communication through the use of text messaging: brackets, colons, smileys and numbers. In early 2009 a report published by Coventry University even appeared to demonstrate that texting, counter to public opinion, has had a positive effect on children's literacy levels; They found that the use of so-called 'textisms' could be having a positive impact on reading development. Dr Beverley Plester, the lead author of the report published in the *British Journal of Developmental Psychology*, concludes that, 'The alarm in the media is based on selected anecdotes but actually when we look for examples of text speak in essays we don't seem to find very many . . . The more exposure you have to the written word the more literate you become and we tend to get better at things that we do for fun.'

The study also found no evidence of a detrimental effect of 'text speak' on conventional spelling, saying, 'What we think of as mis-spellings, don't really break the rules of language and children have a sophisticated understanding of the appropriate use of words.'

This report is not the only one to recently support the positive impact of texting culture. Similar research from the University of Toronto into how teenagers use instant messaging also found that instant messaging had a positive effect on their command of language.

All kinds of recreational activity are also educational

Schooling is in danger of stifling our children's development by forcing them to believe that their cultures and practices are of secondary importance and that they have no value in greater society. The debates that rage about the use of mobile phones and simulation computer games in our schools seem to have no 'grey area', just strong opinion. The truth is they could have tremendous power as vehicles for learning. A report published by education think tank Futurelab in 2006 called *Teaching With Games* concluded that games could improve pupils' computer skills, strategic thinking and problem-solving.

The study, which used games such as Sims2 and Rollercoaster Tycoon, also revealed that games used in the classroom did not have to be fully representative of reality to be useful. A MORI poll taken as a separate part of the project found 59 per cent of UK teachers wanted to use computer games for educational purposes, and that 53 per cent believed games motivated and engaged students.

A few years ago I read an article online published by SLIC Best Practices in Teaching about Second Life, one of the new breed of interactive virtual worlds growing in popularity by the day. Second Life currently has over 15 million registered users. According to this article, Second Life held their first virtual education conference in May 2007, attracting over 140,000 delegates. At this virtual conference a professor of Literature from an Ivy League university explained how she had discovered a faithful reproduction of the worlds of Thomas Hardy in Second Life and how she was now using it to enhance her teaching of classics such as *Tess of the D'Urbervilles*. Inspired, I got my children to help me get set up on the site. Within ten minutes I had discovered the Holocaust Museum, an interactive and totally immersive experience that gave me a new and powerful insight into that particular period of global history. As a teacher I thought of the incredible possibilities this online social network presented.

It is not technology alone that has made a difference to the way our children see or use the world but it has played a significant role in their outlook. They are exposed to so much so young. They witness events and issues in ways that we never did: wars, terrorist acts, sports, celebrities have all been given a new and different reality. I am not sure that as a child I truly understood, or was affected by, the issues surrounding the Cold War in the same way our children are by the war on terror. I certainly didn't know about what Carrie Fisher was having for breakfast or who she was dating with the same clinical insight our children have about Lindsay Lohan. This presents a challenge in itself to the way we frame education and schooling. It means that we must focus on helping our children use technology and their culture to develop a sound and rounded view of the world. We must help them develop the skills and competencies to deal with the information revolution and, most importantly, we must help them to realize that they have the tools and it is our job to help children apply them.

Schooling should be a journey which helps our young develop their interests and cultures responsibly, to see applications and development opportunities that take them beyond what they know, to inspire them to want to know more and, most importantly, to use their experiences to make positive contributions to the global communities they are part of.

Three of the greatest crises facing humanity today – the economic crisis, the environmental crisis, the ethnic and social crisis – were all created by previous generations. Our children are aware of them, frightened by them and feel excluded by them. However, it is their generation that will have to find the solutions if we are to have a meaningful future.

The issues are not whether our children play too many computer games or whether their forms of communicating will undermine traditional literacy. It isn't even whether the minority who are attracted to gangs and youth crime will bring down society. The core concern for us is that we start to understand the impact that 'progress' is having on us and on them. We need to realize that society has evolved as it always does, that with that evolution children have changed, as they always do. Perhaps the difference is the rate at which things have evolved and the complexity that has brought. In many ways our children are already better prepared for the future than we are. They have a greater understanding of the potential of many of the things we fear but they have no idea of how they can use them to protect and develop our societies and cultures. Too many feel excluded and outside of the system for so many reasons.

On the socio-economic front, for example, the Joseph Rowntree Foundation predicted in February 2009 that by 2020 there could be as many as 3.1 million children in the UK living in poverty. These children will have different reasons for feeling excluded from society but the challenge for education remains the same. Up to now we have educated all children with one model, with one set of values and for one perceived purpose; that education is the answer. It can only be the answer if we understand that we are living in a different world and that the education on offer needs to meet the needs of the diversity of society. To do that we must stop believing that education is something that must be done to children and that one size will fit all. We must do more to value children, their cultures and their backgrounds.

CHAPTER 3

Making school matter

Selling school to our children

I have never been very good at doing because I am told to and certainly have always been better at doing because I was inspired to. Education is not a rite of passage . . . to be real it must mean something; it must make us feel better about ourselves and help us to be more complete. It is the greatest of products, the finest of brands – so why do so few of us know this?

Author

We live in a culture where, rightly, education is seen as a right rather than a privilege. However, that same culture believes that children will understand and take up that right because it is there, that they will attend school and learn because it is the law and because if they don't their parents will be prosecuted and taken away by 'the social'. It fascinates me to think that people believe that this will inspire our young to engage in the journey, to embark without fear and with complete enthusiasm on a trip that will take at least 13 years. I am not mad about air travel, but I still get on board and endure ten-hour flights, not because I'm told to, but because I know that I am heading for an experience which will uplift, stimulate and entertain me. Our children do not drive us crazy to cough up our well-earned money to buy them the latest computer game because they have been told they must, but because they want it. Why do they want it? Because successful marketing and the quality of the product are so good that every child and, indeed, many adults feel that ownership will make their lives a little better.

It is simply not enough to build schools, even gleaming new chrome and glass ones and expect our children to flood through the gates and beg to be taught.

If, upon first meeting, I derided all of your interests and told you that they were unimportant, then went on to spend hours telling you about my interests and just how important and significant they were and that, really, my 'stuff' was far more important to you than the 'stuff' you cared about, you would shape an interesting and pretty negative opinion of me. In fact, I am sure that I would fast become a person you would want to avoid at all costs. I would certainly be the last person that you would come to for advice or help. Interestingly, this is exactly what many of us do to our children at school. They arrive filled with interesting and meaningful interests that they want to share and celebrate, toys that inspire them, TV programmes that entertain them, experiences that have captured them and we tell them that we are 'doing work' now, important things, things that matter and that their interests are okay to chat about during break, 'show and tell', or if they are really good and work really, really hard, during 'Golden Time', because they aren't important enough for 'Prime Time'!

This is part of what I call de-contextualizing learning, something our system is effective at and has been for generations. We teach through a series of subjects, fragmented pockets of knowledge bound together by a timetable and exercise books. The vast majority of children don't see school as learning for life, but as learning to jump little hurdles and, like successful Olympians, our highest school achievers learn to play the game and run the race with great timing and confidence. Most still don't know why they are running the race, but someone once told them that if they did well at school, then they would get a great job when they were older. What an interesting discussion to have with a 6 year old. During the research for this book I was not surprised to find little published material which asked young people what they thought school was for. It is not a question asked in official circles very often, possibly because of the candour and discomfort the responses may give, but I did come across a study from the Educational Outcomes Research Unit in Melbourne, Australia from the late 1990s that found that high school students in Queensland, when asked to rank the various purposes of school in order of perceived importance, ranked gaining good academic results at the top of their list, with friendships, personal maturity and learning respect and care for others at the bottom. One boy was quoted as saying, 'They teach Algebra and Maths and stuff like this that we will never use later on in life but they won't teach us about stuff that is important to us and that we should know and learn.'

We should look to the future to define the educational experiences we manage for our children. We must also look to think more creatively about the way we package the learning, to make it exciting, relevant and dynamic. I have often thought that it would be interesting to ask one of the world's giant advertising agencies to create a campaign that marketed learning to children. It fascinates me that in business and industry a considerable amount of time and resource are put into marketing products and services to an organization's customer base and customer demographic. In start-up business 20–30 per cent of total budget is not uncommon, yet in schools we spend no time considering the same scenario. Our children have become complex consumers, some of the most powerful in the global market-place. We must therefore begin to recognize this.

The issue here is not that we have generations of children who don't want to learn, the problem is that they don't want to learn when they can't see the point of the learning. How often did we sit in classrooms and 'do' because we were told to, because we were too afraid not to? How often did we 'do' because we took a particular shine to a teacher and wanted to please them, or get the present promised to us by our parents if we had a good report or parent's evening? This is not what we should be aspiring to for our children; we should be seeking to engage their interest and enthusiasm because they can see the links to their own lives and that by engaging in the journey, they will gain something now and in the future.

I found this sad blog comment recently:

> I have finished education and i feel lost in the world of work i don't have 1 main idea that i want to go on and pursue in my life.

(Posted on The Edge Forum website, August 2008)

When was the last time you learnt something new? Why did you buy this book? My guess is because you thought it would help you understand something you wanted to know about or felt would make your life better. How often do you, in hindsight, think, 'I wish I had known then what I know now. My life would have been so different.'? Surely we do not want our children thinking the same thing in 20 years' time. We want them thinking, 'I am really glad I know this, it's going to make a real difference.' In order for this to happen we must not strive for the status quo. Instead, we need to find ways to make education the new rock 'n' roll. A question I have asked fellow educators many times is, 'Why is school not as exciting as Disney World?' I can hear the laughter now, but why isn't it? Why is it that on a cold February morning, if my child wakes up with a sore throat, they will cough, splutter and act as if they need to be read the last rites, instead of wanting to go to school, yet if they woke up on that same February morning with the same sore throat in Disney World, Cinderella's mice turned horses couldn't keep them away from a day at the Magic Kingdom? Why should school not feel more like that?

Amazing! Engaging students is key to teaching success

Harley Davidson and twenty-first century branding

The world today is dominated by the advertising industry. It employs more behavioural psychologists than any children's services department! On a personal level I hate them and what they do to my kids! They have caused more rows and cost me more money than anything else I can think of since I have had children of my own. But, and I say this with real regret and some hesitancy, I have a grudging respect for what they do and the way they manipulate our children. If we knew how to motivate our children half as well as they do, how powerful could the desire to learn become?

There are some very interesting principles to be learned from the way a company develops and maintains its brand which are best illustrated by the example of Harley Davidson, seen by many in the marketing business as trailblazers for the modern branding magic! They are a company that have, with great skill, developed a brand that transcends their products. While motorbikes will always be the core of their business, the vast majority of their outlets sell fashion items: jackets, t-shirts, jeans and cologne, not motor bikes. In reality they have found the Holy Grail; people buy their logo and advertise the brand for them. Their success is largely down to the fact that Harley stands for a lifestyle, not just the wheels, gears and engine of a high-powered dream machine. Harley stands for freedom, rebelliousness and the American way! A real draw for many and a model that many companies have followed.

Take Nike, so powerful is their identity that a poster with a tick or a swoosh is enough to stir the emotions of their millions of followers. They have spent millions, possibly billions, signing up the greatest sports stars on earth: Tiger Woods, Rafael Nadal, Cristiano Ronaldo and many more in order to promote the 'just do it' philosophy, the belief that Nike stands for world class performance, for winners! Our children and, indeed, many of their parents want t-shirts, hats, anything that bears the 'swoosh' so that they can belong to the brand.

Of course schools neither have the money or indeed the inclination to become Nike or Harley. I'm not sure that I'd be overly happy if my daughter came home with a tattoo of her school crest on any part of her body, as many do with the Harley logo, but there are some fundamental questions that would help us to develop a greater brand identity and an understanding of how to sell it to our customers; our children.

The first question any company must clarify when it is developing its branding is:

What do we stand for in the eyes of our clients/customers?

The second, and perhaps most important, is:

What behaviours do we exhibit every minute of every day to support the brand?

This second question becomes critical and challenging for a school, because all it takes is one member of staff to say the wrong thing in the wrong way, at the wrong time and the brand is in trouble. For example, the battle cry of a particularly pugnacious dinner supervisor, 'Oi, you, get here now!' has a real impact on a school whose brand is one of community, caring and respect.

Perhaps the greatest example of these two questions working brilliantly and disastrously within the same company is the recent experience of the electronics phenomenon that is Apple. The company grew as the antithesis to Microsoft and IBM, the computing brand that stood for individuality, design and customer ownership. It was the brand for free thinkers and creatives, the antidote to the corporate and starchy leviathans in Silicon Valley and, boy, were they successful! That is until they decided to dip their toe in the mobile phone market. When the phone was launched it caused global hysteria, a phone so beautiful, so original that it was an instant classic and so totally Apple, but they made a near catastrophic error in behaviour when they launched the phone, because the brand that stood for freedom of choice, as the opposite of the corporate control of organizations like Microsoft, said that Americans could only buy an iPhone if they signed a long-term contract with one network provider, AT&T. In one ill-judged moment, the company's behaviour threatened the whole brand.

Branding is a complex science but one I believe that schools and people with responsibility for learning must embrace. Children 'opt out' of schooling in many ways; from not doing homework to not concentrating or misbehaving in class. The most extreme opt out is, of course, school truancy. There has been a huge investment – approximately one billion pounds – in reducing truancy in English schools since 1997. There are many reasons for persistent truancy, including low self-esteem, often caused through low levels of basic skills in literacy, bullying and external family issues. Most truancy, however, is because young people feel increasingly that the school experience is irrelevant. In 2008 in England there were over 233,000 children who were classed as persistent school absentees, those missing at least one day of school every week. While the government's investment has shown some signs of working, the figures are not shifting to any meaningful degree and, while the rate of authorized absence is dropping, possibly due to the fact that local authorities and schools now have the power to fine and prosecute families who take unauthorized holidays during term time, the figure of unauthorized absence is rising. There is a worrying pattern emerging. According to 2007 statistics produced by the Department of Education, the average level of absence in secondary schools runs at around 1.42 per cent but by Year 11 (16 year olds) that figure rises to over 2.4 per cent. It does appear that children are voting with their feet.

To understand the branding challenge and where we are going wrong the following advice on branding from The Mud Valley™ Brand Marketing Community may be of interest. They say of branding that:

> Brands win when they create a powerful experience that is totally compelling to the customer, and deliver it better than anyone else. The fewer the people you target with your brand, the more compelling is likely to be your claim in a highly competitive market. The more people you try to capture with your brand, the weaker may be your claim on any given customer, with one exception. In an environment where your customers do not have a relationship with any brands in particular, they will probably be drawn to those they recognize the best. Brands are therefore a bit like light beams. The more concentrated the beam, the more cutting power it will have (as in a laser beam); however, even a diffuse beam, like sunlight, will shed more light and heat than will darkness.

(The Mud Valley™ Brand Marketing Community, 2002)

This brings into focus one of the greatest problems facing the 'education brand'. It has been defused over time, watered down to capture too many stakeholders and, therefore, its vision, its purpose, its brand have become unclear. The fact that education is driven by policy, often to meet political and media-driven means has also resulted in a loss of customer confidence and empathy. After all, who are the customers? Are they the national press, parents, politicians? Surely our customers are our children, as it is they that have to buy into the brand and want the product? When we hear about dealing with truancy we hear about fining and prosecuting parents, of holding schools to account by setting truancy targets. Very rarely do we hear about how we are selling the brand, ensuring its relevance and creating an experience for our children that is powerful and totally compelling. To do that we must have a far greater respect for our customers, seek their opinions and act on their advice. We must make sure that the 'sales people' the teachers, are focused on selling the learning, and making it irresistible. I was recently observing a science lesson in a secondary school where the teacher was asking the children to respond to a series of questions about an experiment on enzymes. When they volunteered their responses the teacher would say, 'That's right, well done, remember it, because it's important. Why is it important? Because it is an A star answer and we should all be looking for an A star in our exams.' For some children that is motivating because their focus comes from the successful passing of exams, for others it wears thin very quickly.

We need to be far more considered in our thinking and the branding of our schools. We need to recognize that our children are the most targeted and, as a result, the most sophisticated consumers ever. We need to respect this and do something to counter it. It is time to swallow our pride and learn how to play the branding game!

CHAPTER 4

The positivity of failure

How making mistakes makes a difference

To be successful you must respect failure and understand the power that not knowing can give you. Very few ever truly aim high enough or realize their potential. The really successful never stop trying, never stop making mistakes and never feel that they have got all the answers. The joy is in the journey.

Author

Our education system is a high-stakes scenario best reflected in the cultural phenomenon that is *Who Wants to be a Millionaire?*, the television game show that challenges people's general knowledge and courage by raising the stakes related to success and failure in powerful financial terms. Do you keep going and risk failure, the loss of everything you have so far gained? Do you chance the next question, the next challenge? You have won £500,000, do you risk it all for a million? If you go for it and you get the answer right, you're rich! If you get it wrong you lose everything! It takes a certain kind of person to take on the challenge, another who is prepared to take a risk that tough and another again to hold their nerve and pocket the jackpot. The programme is a global success. It is hugely entertaining, the main reason being the element of risk, the pressure and emotional strain that that risk exerts, not just on the contestant, but on the audience too.

In many ways school can be like the gameshow. It is a system designed so that we believe that success is measured by the passing of exams and that the most intelligent, talented and capable young people graduating through the system are the ones with the most qualifications and the highest grades. As a result we focus our energy and our time on heading for the jackpot. As children we are told that if we keep climbing the ladder we will end up rich, but if we fail we could lose everything. For some this is fine, they like the game and they are good at it. Others, though, are happy to watch from the safety of their televisions or are so wound up by the risk and the fear of failure that they turn off altogether.

A press release published in 2008 by The Chartered Institute of Educational Assessors found that in a survey of 2,000 adults, 77 per cent felt that their exam results did not reflect their true abilities and that 90 per cent of teachers do not believe that exams are the best indicator of their pupils' abilities. I remember being told as a child that your ability to pass exams and eventually gain a degree demonstrated to future employers your ability to stick to a task, your resilience.

In school how many exams you are taking, how good your results are and how high up in the class you come have a huge impact on your sense of being, of confidence and social standing; it always has done. The levels of self-confidence we carry, the levels of worth and status, have a huge effect on our ability to function well, to be able to interact and to feel involved. Schools are high-risk environments, places where you aren't gambling with money, but with something of far greater value, with self-esteem.

One thing is clear above all else: we live in a society where the risk of failure is seen as something to be avoided at all costs. We live in a world where there are two options: right or wrong, pass or fail. As a result, we are a culture obsessed with winners, a culture that worships and envies winners at the same time. We are a society that derides 'losers'. As a result, very few people take risks, jump in and give it a go.

We are born risk-takers. In fact, we are born as the perfect learning machines. If you think about just how much we learn before we start formal education: walking, talking and toilet training, among many, many other things. We explore as toddlers because everything interests us. Granted sometimes this can be quite dangerous – I still bear the scars from when I learned what radiators do – but we explore and discover because we want to; we don't see the consequences of trying to find out and getting it wrong. Young children have no sense of embarrassment or shame caused by failure. One of my favourite times of the week as a headteacher used to be leading an assembly in my school's infant department (3–7 year olds). I would often start off by saying 'I need a volunteer . . . ' Before I could finish the sentence every hand in the room was in the air. They were almost wetting themselves with excitement and a desire to be chosen; it didn't matter what they were volunteering for, they just wanted to be involved. When I took a junior assembly (7–11 year olds) and asked the same question, I saw before me something reminiscent of a Mexican wave. The younger children would still put their hands up. The older ones were split: some wanted to – you could see it on their faces – but others, who didn't, would stare at them and often persuade them not to put their hands up. This was not through malice, but a reminder that they didn't want to stand out, or worse, be made to look a fool! Taking my assembly road show to my local secondary school, I was met with 'attitude', a defence mechanism that told me in no uncertain terms that, 'I am not sticking out from the crowd. Better not to try than to fail or worse, look stupid!' Sometimes I run professional development seminars for teachers and school leaders, all of whom are highly successful professional people. When I ask for a volunteer, they do everything in their power to avoid eye contact with me. Why is that? What do we do to our young that transforms them over time? If we want to develop a successful education system that truly exposes and develops the potential of every individual and prepares them to lead the challenges of the future, we must work to change the nature of one concept: failure and the notion of risk.

If I have learnt nothing else from my time as a teacher, I have learnt that you learn nothing new from getting everything right. You only ever learn something new when you make a mistake or realize you can't do something.

There are many reasons for under achievement at school and many studies that cite issues related to emotional problems, character clashes with teachers, peer pressure, boredom and a fear of trying. This last one is interesting as it calls into question many of the stereotypes we would assume fit children who potentially may fail: those of low academic ability, poor socio-economic background, boys. Edward E. Jones, a psychologist at Princeton University, says that many 'middle class' children who come from stable homes under achieve at school because of the projected pressures from parents and families – the pressure of expectation – and that many young people become so scared of not fulfilling expectation that they withdraw altogether. A fear of failure is cultivated at all levels and for all kinds of reasons but limited criteria for success and the high stakes that those criteria represent do not help.

Thank heavens the great inventors and innovators in world history didn't think so. They realized that failure, mistake-making, is the most important part of a learning journey, as it is only at the point of making a mistake, or failure, that we can learn anything new. Three great quotes about mistakes and success underline the point:

Do not fear mistakes. You will know failure. Continue to reach out.

Benjamin Franklin

I've learned that mistakes can often be as good a teacher as success.

Jack Welch, Straight from the Gut

The successful man will profit from his mistakes and try again in a different way.

Dale Carnegie How to Win Friends and Influence People

Children are taught to avoid crosses on their work at all costs: right is good, wrong means another playtime doing more of the same. Some may say that that is character forming, the lessons that have built our nation. I would say that it was part of the problem that holds society back. Our obsession with mistake-avoidance and pass and fail is the enemy of a truly successful system.

Parents' evenings are the perfect place to see the misconception of what is important and what isn't, particularly our preoccupation, as parents, with ticks on a page. I have worked with many teachers, particularly in my early years of teaching, who were so obsessed with ticks in a book and the effect they had on parents that they would make children do all of their work in a rough book, correct it and, when it was perfect, children would be allowed to copy it into their neat books for public consumption – oh, the golden age!

As you can imagine, I am prospectively a nightmare parent to have around at my children's parents' evenings. I am not though, thanks to my wife, also a headteacher, who knows what mouthy parents can do for a child's reputation. She holds my hand when we are sitting on those little chairs facing the teacher, knees scuffing our chins. She holds my hand, not out of affection or even as a show of parental unity, but so that, if I take an intake of breath in preparation to speak, she can squeeze very hard and ensure a smooth and trouble-free meeting! Recently though, we were sitting outside our son's classroom waiting for our appointed time. Things were going well, the teacher was only running 45 minutes late, which gave us plenty of time to flick through his work. Seated next to us was a couple whose son is one of our little angel's best friends. They were cooing with joy over loved one's books; Dad said with real pride, 'Look at all of those ticks. I told you he'd get on better with this teacher!' I thought to myself that if that were me and that book belonged to my son, I'd be asking the teacher what she was doing to challenge him, as a page full of ticks told me only that he could do what he'd been asked with ease.

I am not arguing that our children should experience only failure or that success isn't vital but we do need to be very careful about how we balance the two extremes in a child's educational experience.

One of the greatest insights into the power of learning and the critical factors that develop successful learners comes from the work of Professor Guy Claxton and the approach he calls Building Learning Power. He defines the 4 Rs of Learning Power as:

Resilience – being ready, willing and able to lock on to learning.
Resourcefulness – being ready, willing and able to learn in different ways.
Reflectiveness – being ready, willing and able to become more strategic about learning.
Reciprocity – being ready, willing and able to learn alone and with others.

(G. Claxton, 2002, page 40)

Within resilience Claxton cites perseverance as a crucial factor – 'stickability', he calls it. I would agree and have used Claxton's work as a teacher and as a headteacher but I would add that in order to successfully develop all four 'Rs' a student needs high levels of confidence and must not fear learning.

How often do we read in the national press about the tragic young people driven to attempt suicide because they can't bear the thought of underperforming in their exams, of failing their friends and family? Recent figures suggest that in the UK somewhere between 600 and 800 young people between the ages of 15 and 24 take their own lives every year. There is a growing concern about the link between exam pressure and mental health problems in our children.

In June 2006 a study published in *Youth Studies Australia* magazine reported that a survey of Year 12 students (16 year olds) in the state of Victoria had found 1 in 5 students had contemplated self-harm or suicide due to the pressures of Year 12. One in three was severely depressed and 41 per cent experienced anxiety. This is not an unfamiliar story. The Childline service in the UK is reporting year on year rises in the number of children between the ages of 12 and 15 calling in to ask for support and advice in dealing with severe exam stress. Many of these children are, perversely, the same kids labelled as the 'goody goodies' at school, the ones who did everything right, the ones who got ticks in their books and were rewarded for it and the ones who only saw the headteacher for a sticker or a commendation. Yet these are the kids as badly affected by our obsession as those whom we condemn as failures or special needs. It is these children who have no context for the positive nature of mistake-making and it is often these children who find it hard to respond to open-ended problems because they are obsessed with finding the right and wrong.

Education is not about right and wrong and it is not about studying to take exams; it is much more important than that. Educational success should not be measured by the number of ticks on a page or your measured academic prowess. It is about relishing challenges, seizing opportunities and seeing mistakes as significant opportunities for development.

When you hear many of the great entrepreneurs of the twentieth and twenty-first centuries talk about their experiences of developing their wealth and success, most will tell you that it was the businesses they bought or created that failed which taught them the most and laid the foundations for their success. Indeed, the historical figure Barack Obama claims as one of his true inspirations failed in two businesses and had a number of other personal and professional failures and tragedies before his 30th birthday, yet Abraham Lincoln went on to become one of America's greatest presidents. He often said that it was by learning from his failures that he created the recipe for success. It is a view shared by Winston Churchill who once said that, 'Success is going from failure to failure without a loss of enthusiasm.'

I recently heard one of the senior youth coaches at the Lawn Tennis Association talk about the problems with British tennis and the lack of success it has experienced over the last 50 years. Apparently they have been doing a great deal of research recently to understand why it is, that over that time, Britain has produced some of the most talented under-12s in the world, but has seen little evidence of that success among the older and, indeed, professional ranks. One of their most significant findings was that the tennis culture in Britain has seen children play a huge number of competitions and, as a result, has put great pressure on its young players to win. (It seems to be part of our youth sport culture. You have only to stand on the touchline at an interschool soccer match and listen to the abuse and comments coming from parents and coaches to know what I mean.) As a result, players are developing their skills and match experience at a very young age but are unable to reflect on their game, particularly after a defeat, and to develop their tactical game. So they reach an age where they are mentally unable to cope with the game as it develops, unlike children of other nations, who have been given technical and mental coaching ahead of 'win, win, win' experiences, thereby leaving our players lagging behind.

I have started to learn to play golf – what an extraordinary game. One of the first things my coach taught me was to make sure that when I hit a bad shot, which I have to say is 99 per cent of the time, that I don't grip the club harder, which it appears is a natural instinct in golf when things aren't going well. By gripping the club harder your shots become even more erratic. It struck me that the same can be true of being a pupil at school: our children want to do well so they try hard. When they fail, many try harder and harder which, ironically, decreases their ability and sends them into a spiral of decline. I have seen it so often in children who start to under achieve – they find themselves in a vicious cycle.

In many ways schools, classrooms and learning are a little like casinos.

The thing is we don't gamble with money but with self-esteem. Every lesson in every school is a little like roulette: the teacher is the croupier spinning the wheel and rolling the ball. Every time we ask children a question, set them a challenge or ask them to participate in learning we ask them to take a risk, to gamble a little of their self-esteem. Now some kids, the high rollers, will walk into the lesson, brimming with confidence. They bring with them 90 or 100 poker chips of self-esteem, while others walk in with one or two. At the point of engagement we ask our children to place their bets: red or black, odd or even. The high rollers happily chuck down 20 chips because they've got plenty more if the ball doesn't fall in their favour but the kids with one or two can't afford to gamble at all, so they opt out, heads down, disengaging, just wanting the game to end and hoping they will leave with their shirts on their backs.

Critically, as children develop and their self-awareness grows, they become more and more aware of the perceived limitations and lack of value of the chips they carry. Fewer and fewer are prepared to take the risks and play the game until, in adulthood, we see the same problem amplified in many workplaces; unhappy people in jobs they loathe who feel increasingly disenfranchized but unable to find the resource to take control, take a risk, change their lives. There is an absolute imperative that, as they develop, we ensure that children find them-selves able to fail, able to take risks and that they feel positive about both. To do that we need to ensure that they build their poker chip stash and, to do that, the development of self-esteem must be at the very heart of all learning and school development.

How many great talents have had their flames extinguished by the system? How many truly gifted, creative people have left education believing they offer nothing because academia was not their forte? It strikes me that, in many ways, our system is fantastic at teaching children what they can't do, but isn't great at helping them discover what they can.

CHAPTER 5

Who do we create our schools for?

Ensuring that we focus on our children

As far as school goes; we are all experts because we have all been there. As a result, we tend to look at what we think it should be, based on our own experience. The problem is that schools cannot be built on what has worked before; because whether it worked or not, it was of a different time. Schools must be built to prepare for the future, to do that we must be sure that they are designed to educate our children not to serve our own nostalgia.

Author

I love what I do; I believe that teaching is a privilege that carries huge responsibility. In my first year of teaching, a 9-year-old boy in my class taught me the most important lesson I have learnt on my professional journey. He was a truly remarkable child. Gary had dyslexia and dyspraxia and found learning a huge challenge. However, he would never give up. His nature and attitude were extraordinary. I remember halfway through that year the school decided to hold a fundraiser for a well-known children's charity. On the first day of fundraising, Gary brought into school his money box which contained near on £70. He insisted on giving the money to the charity. We checked with his mother, as it was a huge amount of money. She confirmed that was definitely what he wanted to do. He had been saving for a toy but when he'd heard about the children supported by the charity, he became adamant that they needed the money more than he did. Gary was indeed special and he had levels of optimism and resilience that would shame most of us. Gary wanted to work in the sport and leisure industry when he grew up as he was passionate about sport. Many in education gave him little chance because of his difficulties, but Gary went on, got the relevant qualifications and, the last I heard, he was managing a sports centre. He won with his resilience, optimism, amazing people skills and natural charm. On his final day in my class he gave me a present, a small photo frame. On the bottom of the frame was engraved the following phrase: 'To teach is to touch a life forever'. The small, plastic frame still has pride of place in my office.

Despite what the press report and what parents are told, teaching is a profession filled with remarkable, committed people who want the best for the children and young people in their care. It is true that there are some teachers who lack skill and sometimes judgement, but I am yet to meet a teacher who wakes up every morning thinking, 'How great it would be to screw up another life today'! The truth is that we are working in very difficult times. With schools developing as hubs of the community with increasing responsibilities for child care, social and health care, as well as educational development, they have become more and more exposed and pressured by the increasing levels of central government intervention which has, inevitably, led to greater levels of reactive policy implementation and data-driven accountability strands.

In 1988 the government introduced a National Curriculum as part of the Education Reform Act. Its introduction came with two principle aims and four main purposes:

- Aim 1: The school curriculum should aim to provide opportunities for all pupils to learn and to achieve.
- Aim 2: The school curriculum should aim to promote pupils' spiritual, moral, social and cultural development and prepare all pupils for the opportunities, responsibilities and experiences of life.

- Purpose 1: To establish an entitlement.
- Purpose 2: To establish standards.
- Purpose 3: To promote continuity and coherence.
- Purpose 4: To promote public understanding.

The purpose of the National Curriculum was to standardize the content taught across schools in order to enable assessment which, in turn, enabled the compilation of league tables detailing the assessment statistics for each school. These league tables, together with the provision to parents of some degree of choice in assignment of the school for their child, were intended to encourage a 'free market' by allowing parents to choose schools based on their measured ability to teach the National Curriculum.

The National Curriculum was developed in response to a growing concern that learning experiences around the country were variable at best and largely dependent on the quality and skill of individual teachers and that the content was highly varied, meaning that children were leaving school with very different levels of skill and content knowledge. The desire was to create an approach which ensured that every child, no matter where they lived, would receive an equitable experience, an entitlement to learning. The National Curriculum was split into the subject areas familiar to us all from our own schooling, led by English, Mathematics and Science. Experts in each curricular area were asked to devise the content and progression for their subject. The result was, unfortunately, over-complex, unwieldy and as a result undeliverable.

In 2000 a revision followed that tried to streamline the formula. At the same time a new drive for basic skills and standards was introduced in the 'core subjects' of English and Maths, so the government introduced the Literacy and Numeracy Strategies. These new strategies were designed and managed by two new agencies, agencies entirely separate from the government's curriculum authority (the QCA). The strategies were combined under the umbrella of the Primary Strategy in 2003 but still remain separate from the rest of the National Curriculum. This led to a new period of fragmentation, confusion and political power struggles which have hampered schools ever since. There was much to commend about the strategies and the principles of them as, for the first time, teachers had a clear framework that charted progress and a logical, stepped approach to the teaching and learning of key skills which had not been available before. For example, when I trained as a teacher I was taught that the teaching of English was done through 'spiral learning'. My lecturer, an extraordinary character, would perch on the end of an old, wooden lab stool, light his pipe and, after thoughtful pause and dramatic puff, announce that to teach English you ensured that the children had plenty of practice at reading and writing as children improved through repetition. Oh, and a few well-chosen exercises in some well-loved textbooks. Almost overnight schooling changed.

Jean's story

My first job was to teach in an inner-city school in Derby. I was partnered with a teacher with well over 30 years of experience. I liked to kid myself that we were paired together for the same reason that vets suggest to dog owners they should buy a puppy to reinvigorate their ageing pet!

My co-teacher, however, did not need a young hotshot to help her. Jean (names have been changed to protect the innocent) was quite possibly the most elegant teacher I have ever met, the best that 'the old school' had to offer. She didn't walk, she hovered. I never heard her raise her voice; she didn't need to. She commanded just the right levels of respect and fear in the kids, and me, for that matter. She had taught every child's parent, grandparent, aunt, uncle and cousin. Jean had a fantastic relationship with the kids and they loved being in her class. It was like watching an artist at work. Jean's room was next to mine with an interconnecting door between. Working next door to her was a demoralizing experience; her kids were captivated, quiet but always laughing. My kids would look at me with pleading eyes that implored me to be like her. Her secret was actually quite simple: she would introduce the children to different worlds, take them to places they had never been and were unlikely to go.

Every year Jean would base the work around her summer holiday, and she would go to some incredible places, places that were exotic and unobtainable. This was just before the boom in long-haul travel. She visited the Indian Ocean, the Caribbean and all ports in between. The whole year's work would be based on that summer's travels. They did a little Maths but not much, she didn't like Maths very much.

The year's work would always begin with a magical slide show. Her husband was a fantastic amateur photographer and on the Sunday night before the start of the new school year, Jean's husband would select the best and most dramatic images and place them in the slide carousel ready for the eagerly awaited show the next morning. For many of the children it was the highlight of their year and often my most depressing moment. My class would be doing the usual start of year exercise: what I did this summer which, for many of our children, was not a lot but I demanded four sides at least. I was trained to expect high standards! Meanwhile, through the interconnecting door, we could all hear the noises that resembled the eager gasps at a firework display, but magnified hugely as the slides wove their magic.

Things got really interesting the year that Jean and her husband had been to Egypt. The presentation was in full flow when suddenly from the room next door came sounds of chaos and the interconnecting door flew open. In stumbled Jean in a state I can only describe as shell shocked. At that moment I had two overriding feelings: one was professional, 'Poor Jean, I must help out and regain control of her class.'

The other, personal and impish, was the inner smile that my colleague wasn't perfect.

After a cup of tea and a little cajoling we built the story of that fateful day. The day before, Jean and her husband had returned from a family event, later than expected, so Jean's husband had been unable to select the slides for the presentation. As a result, Jean had grabbed the carousel as was and set it up ready to go. We learnt something new about Jean that day. I don't know why, maybe it was in an effort to keep their marriage fresh, but Jean's husband took wonderful, arty and, some would say, tasteful photographs of his wife, topless, in front of scenic and iconic settings from their travels.

Jean's life was never the same after that. Nor was mine; since then I have always prepared my lessons well in advance.

Disaster apart, Jean was like many teachers of her day. Children were everything. The richness of learning was in the experience. With the National Curriculum, this was largely lost.

The old days were far from perfect. In fact, they were guilty of much the government sought to eradicate with the development of a National Curriculum. For example, Jean chose her holidays because there were what interested her and she did not expand children's horizons beyond her own set points.

Some would argue that even in Jean's day schools were structured for teachers and staff first and children second. Jean taught about the things she most enjoyed. Of course the kids loved it but, then, for most it was a romantic escape from their own lives. It wasn't aspirational as it was too far away, but it was fantasy. Was Jean teaching to the needs of the children, with any view to prepare them for their futures? The irony is that, if anything, the system has become even further removed from children. Education policy appears largely to be driven by headline approaches and narrow academic outcomes. The government department with responsibility for schools has a protectionist and introspective approach which is driven by an often naive and disconnected understanding of the challenges facing our children and our schools. It would be fair to say that many government agencies have run almost like closed shops; recycling the same people, with the same perspectives. As with so many areas of public sector departments, education is run with far too many layers of bureaucracy and by too many fragmented groups, all wanting to be heard, valued and prioritized. The impact is that the core focus, children, has been lost in the fog. In the business sector companies have been spending many years developing leaner and more agile structures in the knowledge that the world of today and tomorrow will need organizations that can react and adapt quickly and, most importantly, to ensure that the customer is always at the heart of development. There are some schools too which have, for many reasons, lost the ability to make decisions that put the needs of children first. Many headteachers and governing bodies are under so much pressure from different task masters that, for their own self-preservation, they spend their time trying to keep everybody happy: local authorities, school improvement partners and Ofsted, central government wanting schools to manage extended child care provision, hubs for multi-agency child protection implementation, outstanding financial leadership etc., teachers and teaching unions requiring better working conditions and a better work–life balance, with some teachers wanting the priority to be schools run for their comfort. I have worked with teachers who argue against change because they 'like things the way they are'. As a result children are often way down the pecking order. We must all remember that our clients, our customers, are our children.

In the last few years, educators around the world have learnt so much about the way we learn, the way our brains work and about child development that they have begun to see the dreadful mess that now encompasses our system. Experts such as Howard Gardner and Guy Claxton have taken brain science and developed strategies and approaches that mean we are ready to take the art of schooling to a new level. We are becoming increasingly aware that the problem with the system is the system itself.

Some of the highest performing schools in our national league tables are offering our pupils some of the poorest educational experiences. They themselves have been sucked so powerfully into the no-failure culture that exams and league tables have developed that, as schools, they have become obsessed with maintaining and driving their percentages even higher. Parents have been sold the idea that the better the results the better the school. I have visited many of these institutions and seen what the children in these places are put through, particularly in their final primary phase year. 10 and 11 year olds spending hour after hour, day after day, revising and perfecting their techniques and responses to the questions that will spell success for the school, or otherwise. What kind of experience are we offering our children?

In 2008 the government scrapped testing for 13 year olds because they had come to realize that the tests had stifled schools' ability to develop meaningful learning experiences, develop creativity and, most importantly, focus on the needs of individual children. Sadly they don't seem to think that matters to our 11 year olds as, at the time of writing, tests remain for this age group. The key is that all schools must be accountable, they must ensure that parents receive accurate and rounded information about their children's progress. Schools can do this; most have sophisticated internal assessment and tracking systems in place, systems that were not common in the early 1990s. The real concern around government and testing is that accountability has become the core of all policy. There is an obsession with providing data to ensure that parents have information about school performance. You cannot develop a meaningful and powerful education system around data outcomes; the quality comes from the process not the product. As a result, so much of policy is not about educational value but about a veneer of school quality. How many 10 year olds will look back on their primary school days, ten years from now, and recount with affection their Literacy SATs exam? The tragedy is that schools that run this way know what they are doing and feel trapped by the system. After the tests, at the end of May, those same children are exposed to real, valuable educational experiences that will enhance and develop them. We must search our souls and return to our moral duties. We must ask ourselves, why we are doing what we are doing, who is it for and is there a better way?

The Gate Committee and the spelling test

I believe that our role as schools, as educators, as parents, is to help our children develop so that they are able to reach their potential and be capable of making a significant contribution to the world as successful adult citizens. It is not to use our children to live out our own dreams or to rebalance our own inadequacies. At this stage I want to admit to a level of hypocrisy: my daughter, of whom you heard earlier in the book, was in group four spelling at primary school, the top group! This means that I could hold my head up high at the school gate. I could ask my girl what group this and that child was in, find out that they were not in group four, and give them and their parents that kind of affectionate smile that says that, while I am sure your son or daughter is lovely, they are not in group four. How did she reach the lofty heights? Each week she was given 20 words to learn to spell for her test every Friday. Long, impressive words, way beyond her regular useable vocabulary, words she will not see again until she is writing her inevitable doctoral thesis at Oxford (well, she was in group four). She learnt to spell them during the week; indeed I would not allow her to eat until she had them perfect. She would take her test, score full marks, get a smiley face sticker and return the victor. By the following Monday the words were forgotten because she had a new hurdle to jump. Who are the spelling tests for? I am not sure that they really changed my daughter's life chances. However, I have had parents come in to complain to me because their child's spelling words are not long or complex enough!

Herein lies a significant part of the overall problem. Our children know exactly what school is for and the successful ones know how to play the game. School is about hurdles and first past the post. They must score in their spelling and tables tests, they must achieve the right level in their tests, they must get a smiley face for their story. The next time your child says they have written a story at school, ask them why. You may well get a vacant expression. If you're lucky they will say, 'Because that's what we do on Friday mornings.' Ask them if it was any good. If you get past, 'It was alright', ask how they know. 'Well, I got a sticker.' might be the reply. Shouldn't writing a story be to entertain, to create laughter, tension, excitement? Shouldn't we know we've succeeded because the teacher laughed, cried or was scared witless? Many children see school as a series of challenges set by grown-ups for no other purpose than to pass exams set by grown-ups. Is it any wonder so many opt out at the earliest opportunity?

CHAPTER 6

What matters most?

The knowledge vs skills debate

It is time to grow up; to stop battling with our egos and our wit and start to look for a system that suits its purpose. Our opinions are all valid, as are our concerns. Our children need experiences that open their minds to all opportunities and approaches . . . in truth there is no one answer, one right or wrong.

Author

Throughout the history of modern education there has raged a huge debate that questions the focus of the learning journey. In one camp sits those who view schooling as the acquisition of knowledge, knowledge that fires the thirst and enquiry in young minds that then seeks to explore further knowledge. It is the traditionalist. The view that knowledge is power, that IQ is the prerequisite intelligence of learning prowess and, ultimately, success. It clearly views school as a knowledge-currency kingdom.

The other camp argues that, while knowledge is part of the process, it is not the aim; it is a product of the wider system. It argues that the key to success as learners is to develop and hone the skills needed to be successful students. It argues that the role of schools is to prepare children to meet the open-ended problems of their life journeys. The curriculum must be seen as an expansive experience that encompasses every moment of a child's experience in school. It should not be constrained by the notion of timetable and lesson chunks. It is an interesting thought that the only valid learning occurs in classrooms lined with desks fronted by a teacher and in hour-long segments. This is the camp of the progressive.

Of course in truth, great learning, a powerful education, is built on the acquisition of information, of experiences and of skills. It also means that knowledge itself has a fixed and limited definition, that it is simply the acquisition of facts and information. If this is knowledge then it can be deeply unsatisfying if it doesn't stimulate interest or a resonance and often becomes temporary. On the other hand, if we don't have a level of basic skill – reading, writing, control of number – we will find it hard to develop concepts, ideas, deep learning and cognition.

Some of the best explanations of where skills and knowledge fit within cognition can be found in the work of Kim Vicente and Jens Rasmussen in Demark in the late 1980s and early 1990s who, in their work around human behaviours (Ecological Interface Design), talked about the Skills, Rules Knowledge framework (SRK) which was produced by Rasmussen in 1983 to define certain elements of human cognition. It states that there are three ways in which information is absorbed and understood:

Skill-based level

A skill-based behaviour represents a type of behaviour that requires very little or no conscious control to perform or execute an action once an intention is formed. For example, bicycle riding is considered a skill-based behaviour in which very little attention is required for control once the skill is acquired.

Rule-based level

A rule-based behaviour is characterized by the use of rules and procedures to select a course of action in a familiar work situation. The rules can be a set of instructions acquired through experience or given by supervisors and those with previous experience.

People are not required to know the underlying principles of a system to perform a rule-based control. For example, hospitals have highly proceduralized instructions for fire emergencies. Therefore, when one sees a fire, one can follow the necessary steps to ensure the safety of the patients without any knowledge of fire behaviour.

Knowledge-based level

A knowledge-based behaviour represents a more advanced level of reasoning. This type of control must be employed when the situation is novel and unexpected. People are required to know the fundamental principles and laws by which the system is governed. Since people need to form explicit goals based on their current analysis of the system, cognitive workload is typically greater than when using skill- or rule-based behaviours. (J. Rasmussen, 1983, pages 257–266)

While this is a distillation of what is complex and provocative work, it helps shed some light on what has been a drawn-out, and often apparently unsolvable, stand-off. The idea that a skill is a function; a process which, once learned, can be applied automatically. Take walking, for example. It cannot, on its own, drive a person on to greater things, to new discoveries or learning, but it is a vital component. So, as we walk, if we add the level of rules, then we know that walking on a pavement or in a pedestrian area, rather than in the road, is safe. We can now apply that skill with some confidence but it is still just walking. It is only by adding the third level, knowledge, that things really hot up because now we know what route to take to get to the riverside because we remember landmarks and pathways. Our skill, our rules and our knowledge can take us to a place where we can develop new thinking and immerse ourselves in new experiences and that will then spur us on to keep walking.

In truth, one level without the others can be sterile and to an extent meaningless. When I first came across Rasmussen's levels what struck me is that most 'traditional' schools don't operate at the skills or the knowledge levels at all but at the rules level. As pupils we learn the routines, the systems, the criteria for success and failure and then operate almost automatically within that level. I have seen so many children and, indeed, teachers operate here. Therefore the real challenge and debate need to be around the balance and emphasis of where we fall as schools and the strategies we need to develop to work through all three stages.

The Royal Society for the Encouragement of the Arts, Manufacture and Commerce (the RSA) in 1999 produced an alternate picture of a curriculum for the twenty-first century called The Opening Minds New Curriculum. It was designed as a reaction against the, by then revised but still highly prescriptive and overly detailed, National Curriculum. The RSA argued that the National Curriculum was not going to meet the needs of children in the twenty-first century, as it was dominated by a knowledge-driven approach which continued to feed the Victorian view. Unfortunately the work of the RSA, which was of huge merit and considerable importance, was rubbished by some facets of the establishment.

It was designed as an alternative approach for children from 11–16 years. However, the climate, together with the derisive sneering of the ill-informed civil servants driving the government's agenda, meant that the project was largely ignored and deprived of credence. As a result, it resided on the RSA website for many years. I discovered the project in 2002, thanks to some work I was doing with the Innovation Unit. It is an immensely thought-provoking piece of work and has huge resonance now more than ever. The project argues and demonstrates that the current curriculum, because of its knowledge-drive, is failing to address and develop the significant levels of skills needed for our youngsters to thrive in their adult lives. It includes sections on developing not just learning skills, but handling mass data and, significantly, a growing financial awareness. Interestingly, the material is enjoying a strong resurgence since the publication of Every Child Matters, as many schools are discovering its relevance and applying its principles. The website is now alive with case studies and exemplars and in his 2009 report to the UK government regarding the reforms in primary curriculum, Sir Jim Rose recommends that government agencies work closely with the RSA to develop new skills-driven frameworks.

The view of the work exemplified by the RSA was also reflected in the All Our Futures report, which was the result of an enquiry set up by the government to explore education, employment and the importance of creativity. The report, whose committee was chaired by Professor Sir Ken Robinson in 1999, was developed by a leading panel of experts from the fields of education, science, the arts and industry. The report concluded that creativity and the arts needed to be developed throughout the curriculum and that inspection systems and teacher training needed to reflect a greater emphasis on the development of skills and competencies that allowed for the explicit development of creative process in all of our children. While the then Minister of State for Education and Employment, David Blunkett, responded to the report in some detail, which led to some powerful commitments and initiatives, namely around music education and the development of creative partnerships, the report's key recommendations around curriculum, assessment, teacher training and inspection remained somewhat unheeded. Maybe the timing didn't help, given that the Department of Education had just completed its major review of National Curriculum. Maybe the recommendations were too challenging politically. What is significant is that the profession still sees the All Our Futures report as the seminal commentary on the future vision for future schooling. Interestingly, the powerful commitments and initiatives that were acted upon were largely implemented through the Department of Culture, Media and Sport, not the Department of Education.

The fact that the government seem to be able to separate so neatly the skills, competencies and experiences that develop our creative potential from what they consider to be the clear priorities of education is worrying but, to an extent, matches the Rasmussen material and appears to demonstrate that the education system is clearly defined by the rules-based level.

I recently read a book by Caroline Taggart called *I Used to Know That*. The book is filled with facts and information that we spent our school days trying to learn and remember. In her introduction the author says that she had forgotten at least 90 per cent of everything she had included in the book. It strikes me that, as a hugely successful author, editor and publisher, she has done okay!

It would seem that one of the greatest problems in a debate that pits knowledge against skills is that people do not have clarity of understanding around the term 'knowledge'. It is clear that Rasmussen sees knowledge as far from static or a series of facts or compilations of information. Knowledge as a term has had a complex history debated and defined by figures such as Plato, Aristotle and Descartes but for me the clearest definition is that:

> Knowledge evolves. So far we may understand it as accumulated external and explicit information belonging to the community, being leveraged by tacit intrinsic insights which originate within individuals who then may act alone or cooperatively in order to control or integrate with their environment.
>
> *(M. K. Fletcher, 'Guidelines for Knowledge Management from the Phenomenological Literature', 2002)*

What is clear is that knowledge is not a fixed entity and that the acquisition of knowledge relies on a number of skills and intelligences that help process information and experiences, drawing on previous contexts and then questioning to find meaning from those experiences and information. For example, it is a fact that Anne Boleyn was executed on 19 May 1536 and that is of temporary interest to most. To have knowledge around this fact would require a person to be able to understand the context and reason for the execution and then to use that information to form an opinion. This of course takes previous facts, knowledge and understanding. It also, crucially, requires a level of interest in the facts in the first place and that means that they must have relevance.

One of the key issues of a curriculum that is defined by its content, by facts, is that it fires a debate around what facts should be taught and when. As a result, we end up with fierce and often emotive arguments about who and what children should learn about and what it is important for them to remember. As a result, we end up reading headlines in newspapers which say that children will no longer be taught about Winston Churchill or that children can't remember the dates of the Great War. The point is that simply 'knowing' is not what children should be doing; that is not the acquisition or development of knowledge. What we want is for children to develop a knowledge and understanding of great leadership and how Churchill exemplified that by leading the Allies. If what we obsess about are the facts and the ability to memorize then our system will continue to produce Caroline Taggarts; people who have forgotten most of what they learnt at school. In truth, the acquisition of knowledge requires great skill.

Building buggies

One of the most popular Design Technology projects run in schools is to design and build buggies. It is a wonderfully adaptive task that can fit any topic, but the joy is that the basic components are the same. Like a great *Blue Peter* challenge, the resources are cheap and accessed through household junk, some card, old cotton reels, glue and a little dowel. Once mastered, buggies can become Roman chariots, Stuart coffin carts or gypsy caravans. It is one of those projects the children tend to love and the teachers plan a month before a parents' evening, as the results look wonderful on display.

The sessions begin with an in-depth explanation from the teacher on how to plan your buggy, in this case a moon buggy, which joining techniques to use and how to ensure that the mini hacksaws cut only wood and avoid flesh. He, or she, will spend an hour showing children how to cut, paste and colour the buggies so that they look just so. The children will marvel at their teacher's dexterity and making ability.

Having spent the best part of an hour demonstrating and constructing, the teacher is nearly ready to allow the children to begin. Technology usually stretches for a double period of an afternoon, because most teachers can only bear the mess and disruption once a week, so getting it over with in one hit is always the best option. Just before sending the children to break for 15 minutes, the teacher, having seen a good opportunity for some team working, wants to get the children working in groups of four. So the teacher, in the two minutes before break, tells the children of the plan and asks them, as quickly as possible so as not to detain them from the playground, 'How do we work best in teams?' The children respond by proudly raising their hands in the air. Little Josh is the child invited to respond, 'We take it in turns to talk around the group so that we all get a chance to make suggestions and we don't make too much noise.' With that, breaktime can begin and the children begin construction upon their return.

Buggy construction is fun and of educational benefit, but in the future lives of our kids, which will be of more importance: building a buggy or really learning how to work within a team and applying the skills needed to build something? Knowledge of how to work in an effective team requires a very complex set of skills, learnt over time. We must know our own strengths and weaknesses, understand how to share and identify the same in each other, know what makes good team dynamic and how to utilize each other's strengths to the best advantage. For example, the chatty child has a role to drive the group forward, the child obsessed by detail becomes the questioner and the child who likes organization charts the group and keeps it on track.

The National Curriculum does not focus on these skills or, indeed, demand that they are covered. So much of what is really important is left to chance, is seen as a by-product. Imagine the power of a curriculum that puts the life and learning skills of children at its heart and uses concepts and information as the tools to exemplify and provide experience.

The education system is obsessed by outcomes. It measures quality through product, not through process. As a result, the quality of the journey is seen as secondary to the result and that there is little time for the development of knowledge in its truest sense. This leads to a blinkered and predefined approach that narrows possibilities and leads to the system that our children inhabit, a system stuck in its own traditional quagmire, a system rooted in the ghosts of the past, not the projections of the future. The very skills we know we have to develop and nurture in our children do not fit into an information-based curriculum that is defined by 'you either know it or you don't.'

We are currently in the depths of one of the world's greatest financial crises, a crisis that will change the nature of work and capitalism forever. Many experts believe that the future of the West lies in the development of entrepreneurship. It is a view that I have heard expressed by some of the UK's most successful business people, including Sir Richard Branson, in a speech he made in Johannesburg in 2009. In 2008, two of the entrepreneurs made famous by the BBC television series *Dragon's Den* launched books about their lives. In interviews at the time, both Duncan Bannetyne and James Caan said the same thing; they had failed at school and were not considered clever. With a combined wealth of nearly half a billion pounds, I reckon that their teachers were wrong!

Information can only be power if you have the skills to use it to develop your journey and turn facts into knowledge. Also, knowledge is only powerful if it is important to you and your context, otherwise it becomes nothing but trivia. In theory, in the future, if our system remains largely unchanged, our children may be coming top in their local pub's quiz league but we need to develop innovators, leaders and creative thinkers, not trivia experts. We need a curriculum that works toward that goal; we need to move way beyond Rasmussen's rules-based level to explicitly develop a marriage of skills and relevant knowledge, to apply knowledge in contexts that fire the imagination and stimulate a desire to explore further. After all, moon buggies would be useless without the creativity, innovation and application of the skill, creative thought and ability to ask the 'What if?' that lead to space exploration.

CHAPTER 7

The world beyond the gate

Creating real contexts for learning

> The truly great school is one that recognizes that it does not house the font of all knowledge, kept safe behind a gate through which only the chosen can enter. It realizes that it is a delta from which many tributaries flow for all to explore.
>
> *Author*

Whether we like it or not, the world has changed and so have children. The one fundamental change between 'now' and 'then' is the exposure to the world through the growth of mass media. It is not all good; in fact much is very worrying. Sadly, childhood seems to have disappeared in many ways. Our children are aware of so much more in the world than ever we or any previous generation were. They have access to levels of knowledge and experiences that were beyond us until well into our adult lives. They also have greater levels of disposable income than ever we did, something that advertising companies and the businesses that employ them are only too aware of.

Our kids want to be grown-up so badly and, like all children of every generation, they mimic the actions of their role models to appear mature and adult. In my generation the cigarette was the symbol of being adult, and sometimes a little alcohol. The problems caused by the evolution in media trends and technologies are massive, but one thing we know is that they won't go backwards. Pandora's Box has been opened and closing it again is impossible. We cannot ignore the developing world, or try to sweep it under the carpet. Our young have become such self-aware individuals that to do so creates new taboos and, as we are all aware, there is nothing more enticing for young minds than the challenge represented by challenging adult-defined taboos.

We live in a world where a pretty, blonde teenager can walk into a house loaded with cameras a 'nobody', and walk out a matter of weeks later a superstar, reputedly having earned a million pounds and a modelling contract. Recent articles in the press – including a 2005 *Manchester Evening News* article entitled 'Naked Ambition Rubs Off on Teenagers' and a *Daily Mail* article called 'We Want to be Jordan' (17 July 2008) – estimate that around two- thirds of teenage girls aspire to become glamour models. We live in a world where some of our children believe that 'gangsta' culture is the ultimate form of expression and rebellion.

We cannot ignore the influences on our young. It is clearly not going to be enough to tell them to avoid the influences and hope to convince youngsters that they are wrong. We must do more, much more to help them understand the world they are growing into.

This world is not only fraught with danger, but also with an abundance of experiences that, if shared well, can lift learning and child development to new heights. It is our responsibility as educators and parents to work hard to find the positive routes that not only help prepare our children for the minefield, but help them to contextualize their place within it.

In schools we ignore the modern world at our peril, paying lip service to the rate of technological change with some interesting gadgets and computer ratios. We have been forcing children to leave their interests and cultures at the gate. Certain elements of society hope that by pursuing a traditional curriculum we can show children the errors of their ways and the futility of their developing cultures.

Alistair Smith, founder of the education consultancy ALITE and one of the world's most eminent experts on child educational development and media culture, alerted me to a wonderful quote that beautifully illustrates the problem we face. It comes from an article in the *Daily Mail* in 2005. The article was berating the fact that some schools were pushing media studies courses at GCSE and A level with equal fervour as the more traditional subject of English Literature. The article, written by Sarah Harris, contains a quote from the then director of the Campaign for Real English, Nick Seaton.

Media studies is undoubtedly a Mickey Mouse subject,' he said. 'It's obviously designed to be relevant and appealing to young-sters, but it's unlikely to do them much good in later life.

'Some knowledge of the classics is essential for everyone if they are going to be successful in the world

(*'Schools Axe English Lit for Soft Media Studies'*, The Daily Mail, *12 June 2005*)

Is Mickey Mouse not one of the most recognized and celebrated brand icons of the twentieth and twenty-first centuries? Indeed, is Mickey Mouse not now a classic in his own right? Oh, that my daughter should create the next Mickey Mouse!

Basic skills are still an important foundation

I have no argument that the classics are of value and interest. They can transport us to other worlds, stimulate our thinking and demonstrate the richness and diversity of language across the globe. However, I would also argue that new media and an understanding of those media have far more immediate relevance to our children and their futures. We may not feel comfortable with the fact that our world today is controlled by the media, but that is how it is. The internet has changed the planet forever. The only way we can ensure that, for the most part, the extraordinary evolution and development of our planet and its new technology resources are used for good is to ensure our children understand them and can see how to use them constructively. To dismiss them as irrelevant, like some playground fad, is grossly irresponsible, short sighted and downright dangerous.

In many ways this brings us to the crux of our argument. Education and the crucial decisions taken about its future are largely taken by civil servants, based on their interpretation of public opinion. It is easy to pass off anything you do not understand or see a need for in your life as unnecessary, as dangerous and to be avoided. The challenge is to accept the future and to use it to drive forward generations to do well and to improve the world they inherit.

I saw a wonderful item on the BBC News recently about a pensioner who, having discovered video blogging, was using the medium as a platform to air and share his memories and thoughts on the world around him. He had built up a huge following, having received well over half a million hits in a matter of weeks. Many of his greatest fans were under the age of 21.

No-one is saying that the classics are no longer of value, or that traditional skills are of no interest, but many traditional methodologies are outdated.

Our children come from the high-definition, digital, on-demand generation, yet some of our teaching and curriculum remains 14 inch, mono-sound and black and white.

Nothing illustrates this better than the use of technology in our schools. Again, decisions and influence on what our schools should use come from the type of person who is like everyone's favourite uncle, the family member still marvelling over the digital watch. These 'experts' see things like projectors and interactive whiteboards and proclaim them the future of learning, They have told us that ratios of computers of 1:7 or even 1:4 are the future, that fully resourced computer suites, complete with broadband, will revolutionize our system and dazzle our kids with technology that will sell the learning experience. It is now reported that schools spend over half a billion pounds a year on IT equipment in the UK. Have they seen our kids lately? They are working on 'fully loaded' mobiles, allowing them not just video facilities, but the ability to watch their favourite television programmes. They allow our kids to surf the net on demand, carry thousands of their favourite songs and Bluetooth each other across a classroom. Our kids, ten years ago, may have been dazzled but today we are way behind their technological capacity. The computing power in their hands is greater than that of the systems that sent man into space. We shouldn't be banning this technology in our schools. I heard a great quote from a child recently who said, 'Stop trying to teach us ICT. We know more than you, live with it!'

By using the cultures of our kids and the technologies they understand, we could transform our system and drive education into the future.

In his book, *Everything Bad is Good for You*, Steven Johnson argues that programmes like *The Simpsons* are based on the same complexities as some of the great classics to which Nick Seaton refers. They are filled with subtle and ironic inferences, they parody modern society and, as result, are filled with humour and are popular beyond belief. The real triumph is that they are cross-generational. Now imagine the learning involved for our kids if they were taught how that was achieved.

Paragraphing – making it real, making it matter

In a teacher's life there are certain concepts that fill them with dread. Moments within the essential curriculum that will lead to the pulling out of hair and the increase in wine consumption. Of these, teaching children the grammatical understanding of paragraphing ranks high. Paragraphs have always been an abstract concept for kids, but as children read less, the concept is becoming increasingly distant. Packaged tightly in the realms of the Literacy hour, paragraphing relies heavily on set texts to exemplify strategy. To children, the whole thing is seen as a technical skill, for which they see no purpose or benefit. However, children do become experts very quickly, thanks to their understanding of playing the game. Our kids see endless texts where paragraphs are defined by the occasional missed line and indent. They soon realize a visual ratio, that to them defines the paragraph, and very quickly feel that they have found a shortcut to mastering it. Proudly, children will tell you that they are using paragraphs. In their minds, they use the visual cue – usually 4–5 lines of text seem a good length for a paragraph – and visually a missed line at this juncture cements the image. 'Thank you very much', thinks the child: 'kerching', a smiley face and a couple of team points and we can move on to colons.

Sadly, this is the view most children take to the twilight world that is grammar and punctuation. It is not taught in ways to help our children see the context or purpose. We use set texts and books defined by 'experts' to suck children into understanding. The problems are found at this point: first, telling a child that something is great, because it is great, is not helping. To most children, the majority of texts are remote and not worth the effort, so they see paragraphing as a skill that will not be of benefit, as they are never going write books. Secondly, children do understand the abstract concept of paragraphing, they just don't realize it and, more sadly, neither do we.

Take for example, an episode of *Eastenders*, or any other popular soap opera. Like it or not, the vast majority of our children are hooked.

If you were to use a 15-minute clip and stop the film every time the cameras switched from one set or scene to another and ask the children why the camera had done that, the children would look at you as if you were stupid, smirk in that way children can and tell you that the camera had moved to a new destination because we were now watching a different part of the story and different characters. In other words, you tell them, we have changed the focus for the people watching and the camera change has helped us to understand that we are now dealing with something different. 'Yep,' will chime your kids smugly, having taught you something. 'In writing,' you might say, 'we can't use cameras to help the reader, so instead we use paragraphs. Imagine that the next time you write a story, you want to help the reader change focus when you begin a new part to your story, or return to an earlier event. Miss a line at the point that you would expect the camera to take you to a different place.' 'Oh now we get it.' chime the kids, 'Why didn't you tell us that in the first place?'

The staffroom mafia

All schools have them, staff who are sure that the children are out to get them, convinced that children don't understand on purpose. They are most commonly sighted in school staff rooms, often at Friday lunchtime. Most of the staff have just collapsed for 15 minutes respite, to wolf down a sandwich and muster their thoughts for the weekly 'finishing-off session'. The week-long crispbread and decaf coffee good intentions have given way to medicinal chocolate cake and full-octane Nescafé. One teacher has started to inspire visions of the adult world weekend, than the mafia boss announces themselves . . . the staffroom door flings open, a deep sigh fills the room and the figure at the door eclipses the light. The rest of the staff look at each other with defiant stares that say, 'Don't you dare ask them what's wrong!' With increasing frustration, the mafia boss bristles over to the tea- and coffee- making facilities and proceeds to make the loudest cup of coffee ever. The clinking of metal on china chips away like Chinese water torture until eventually one colleague cracks, desperate for the punishment to end. 'What's wrong?' they ask with insincere concern. Mafia boss spins and like a high-powered rifle explodes, 'Those little bastards will be the end of me!' Hopeful smiles pass across the room. Mafia boss is too tightly coiled to notice, 'I have spent all week on full stops and capital letters. We have done exercise after exercise. Yesterday, the little sods had got it. Today, today, we did some free bloody writing and not one of the little buggers has put a full stop or capital letter anywhere.'

The staffroom mafia boss epitomizes the problem: we teach in fixed chunks, information, skills and concepts ring-fenced into defined sections. We, as teachers, are delivering a curriculum filled with sound bites and experiences that mean nothing to our children. The sheer quantity does not allow us the time to mix the recipe, to blend the ingredients together in order to make sense of the whole. This is a bit like telling kids that yeast is important to making bread, but not explaining how to use it in the process. Maybe, more pointedly, children don't see the need to know about yeast anyway, because they buy their crusty batch loaf from the supermarket, hot and ready to eat.

To our children, learning is seen as something they do at school. It is, in a way, role play, make believe, it is a distraction from their real lives. When they look beyond the gates, they don't see timetables, subjects, paragraphs and full stops; they see a huge, glistening, confusing world. They do not see how, by engaging in one, you can understand the other. They feel that they leave real life at the gate. It is our job to move schools forward so that they are seen by our children as a development of their real lives.

CHAPTER 8

The industrial model of schooling

Why our system is out of date

Our children are organic, they are not machines. Productivity does not increase because the conveyer belt is made to run faster or because we create tougher production targets.

Author

So here we are in the early years of the twenty-first century, working on a curriculum that is based on a model at least 200 years old. We define our educational experiences by subject; Music, Art, History, English, Religious Education, Geography, Science, Mathematics, Physical Education, Foreign Languages. We occasionally become modernist and add something 'new wave' like ICT (Information Communication Technology) or PSHCE (Personal, Social, Health and Citizenship Education) or we rename subjects with catchy terms like Numeracy instead of Maths, Literacy instead of English, but, essentially, the world turns and we learn about life and the challenges of our future in bite-size, categorized chunks. Our days are defined by timetables, predictable and ordered. Occasionally, if we are really lucky and usually toward the end of a term, we get something different, like a drama group coming in to do a play about recycling, which means no Literacy or Numeracy on Wednesday morning.

This world has a hierarchy, as Sir Ken Robinson explains in his book *Out of Our Minds*. If challenged to place the subjects in order of importance, we would all end up with similar results. English and

Maths at the top, PE and Music at the bottom. Why? Are they not all connected? To be good at one, you need to be good at the other. The Beatles' music would be half-baked without their lyrics, their lyrics boring without their music, music defined by rhythm and pattern, made rational through an understanding of mathematics.

When you head off to work in the morning, in the car or on the train, and you are listening to the local news, does the announcer say, 'In Maths today, share prices dropped by .6 per cent and in RE, the Bishop of Westminster has expressed his concern at falling church numbers?'

When you get to work, is your work schedule split by subject?

9:30am mtg. with MD, bring English skills for some speaking and listening.

10:30am Ad campaign debrief use Art exercise book

The meeting after lunch presents a problem because it's with the human resources department and is about proposed staff cut. Now is that Numeracy, PSHCE, Literacy or ICT?

Perhaps the answer to the future is already staring us in the face. The most powerful learning environments in our schools currently are to be found in the schooling of our youngest children, known as the Foundation Stage. It comprises Nursery and Reception classes made up of children of 3–5 years old. They run a very different curriculum to the main National Curriculum, based around key learning themes:

- Personal, Social and Emotional Development
- Communication, Language and Literacy
- Problem-Solving, Reasoning and Numeracy
- Knowledge and Understanding of the World
- Physical Development
- Creative Development

As a result the children are given broad learning opportunities, often role play-based, that encompass the skills required throughout the learning journey. So, for example, a key theme may be health and fitness and the children will have activities planned that wrap all of the traditional subjects in a contextual experience. So physical development will involve the children working out to a Jane Fonda video while designing their own 'keep fit' poster and counting the number of steps Jane Fonda uses in her exercise routine.

*Physical exercise can be creatively incorporated
into all curriculum areas*

The best-run Foundation Units are a joy to behold and exemplify the greatest learning platforms. The children are not just happy but confident, self-managing, resilient and creative; they are able to hypothesize and investigate and learn at an extraordinary pace – everything any teacher at any stage or phase would want of their students. We move from this model when children reach 5 and head towards 'proper learning environments,' with desks and chairs and timetables defined by separate subject. This system is refined so that by the time children reach 7, they can tell you what they will be doing Thursday fortnight at 10:15am. Not only that, but lesson structures have become so prescriptive due to the government frameworks, that the children will be able to tell you where they will be sitting and what part of the lesson they will be doing, 'If it's 10:15am, Mummy, we will be in Literacy and we will be just about to go from our activity to the plenary, which is the bit where the teacher asks us to come out to the front and tell the class what we have done and learnt in today's lesson. I won't be doing that bit though, I'll be on the carpet listening, because on Thursdays Butterfly group is chosen to talk about their work and I'm in Ladybirds.'

By the time children are 11, they are facing structure fatigue caused by the monotony of the predictable. So it continues through secondary school, becoming a more and more defined, divorced series of lessons. Why is that the way our system is still defined? In recent times there have been attempts to challenge the status quo. The reviews of primary and secondary curricula developed over the last few years have sought to question subject structure and the single-subject format but they have never been really championed at government level.

Learning should be an expansive, personal and unpredictable journey. Web-based search engines are the perfect example. We Google something and are so fascinated by the new threads the search throws up that, after an hour of exploration, we have forgotten what it was we were originally looking for. Of course we know that ideologically this would be wonderful, but in reality we are restricted and moulded by the exam systems that ground the journey and force narrow and closed routes upon us . . . go explore the world however you want, but you must be home for tea and I will expect postcards from Beijing and Wellington.

I know that this is becoming a recurring theme but the current political fixation with targets and league tables is having a real impact on the quality of education for our children and not in the way our government tells us. Schools are so restricted by the impact that data have on our systems that, in England, schools are educating children in a climate of fear. I firmly believe in accountability and the right of parents to understand the quality of experience their children receive. Our kids only get one chance; each precious day will never come again, so every day must be filled with opportunity and the joy of discovery. Our children are the most precious parts of our lives and we have a right to know that each of them is getting the very best start and the finest quality of schooling.

Ironically, the testing regime and the huge data generated from it are not doing that, they are having the reverse effect. It does, however, usefully employ thousands of people, costing massive sums of money which, if invested in our schools directly, would have a significant impact. As an example, in 2009 the contract for the testing 11 year olds is likely to be worth in the region of £26 million.

It is not only schools that are suffering as a result of the system. Local authorities are forced and pressured to achieve county targets which, in turn, means that the vast majority of their resources and advice must go into short-term advice for schools to raise results. I was employed by a local authority a few years ago and my brief was to work with teachers working with test-age children and to give them techniques to improve results by the end of that year. Sadly this kind of work is of no benefit to our children in the long term; it serves only to fuel statistics.

I am not writing this book as a political statement decrying the policy of one political ideology over another. I believe that this ill-informed obsession goes back generations and is cross-partisan. There are signs that things may change but, whatever happens, politicians must realize that education policy must not be designed to ensure the production of data – education is about the development of children.

The whole testing regime in primary education has been extra-ordinary. Successive governments point to the dramatic increase in results since the system was first introduced in the early 1990s as a vindication of the process. The truth however, is that schools learnt to 'play the game'. When we first put our children through the system we did not know what to expect as teachers, and, therefore, to an extent, our pupils took the tests 'blind'. As a result, for the first couple of years, our children were performing poorly, with just over half achieving appropriate levels. As we, as teachers, became used to the format and the systems we were able to train our children to take the tests, like laboratory rats.

The government then began to formally train us to train the children to take tests, investing a fortune in 'booster classes' and specialist booster programmes. There is no doubt that test results have improved dramatically and that schools, teachers and pupils have worked incredibly hard to see that happen. How much of that is down to the quality of learning and the educational experience is highly questionable. The fact that we have improved test technique and prepared our kids better to take the tests is certain.

Some years ago I was at a meeting when the then Minister for School Standards, David Miliband, was asked to define standards in school terms. He responded that standards were about the preparation of pupils for future, successful citizenship. He was absolutely correct, but standards as defined by tests and league tables are not in any way measuring a school's success in these fields. If you walked in to any Year 6 class in the land in March/April, you would see children devoting every timetabled hour to test preparation. Neither the children nor the teacher would be able to really explain the educational benefit.

We have been sold an educational myth by successive governments that has led to some of our highest performing schools in the league tables offering some of the worst educational experiences for our children in order to play the game. I have heard local authority advisors tell schools to cancel school plays, sporting events and visits in order to spend more time preparing children for the tests.

Although we live in a world where corporal punishment for pupils has been outlawed, the government have discovered new canes to beat them with.

So what are the alternatives? First, of course, there is Ofsted, the government's school inspection agency, which itself has its hands tied by the fact that largely its judgements must be based on data. In one of our school inspections the team made a judgement on the quality of our science teaching based on results over a year old, rather than on the quality of teaching during inspection. As a result they deemed the science to be in need of improvement. One week later we received the latest test data which showed that 100 per cent of our children had achieved the required levels, immediately rendering the inspection judgement worthless. Inspection, if managed properly, is an excellent form of accountability monitoring, particularly if you remove the reliance on crude data. So the possible solution lies in finding an alternative form of data measure.

The government themselves have a growing awareness of the problems within the system, but find themselves trapped in a vicious cycle. Investment in the testing system has been, and continues to be, huge. That investment has been both financial and political. They realize that the system is holding back genuine school development and through documents and strategies introduced in the last ten years, such as Excellence and Enjoyment, Personalized Learning and, most significantly, Every Child Matters are trying to encourage schools to develop more expansive thinking. The problem is that with the regime of testing as it stands, schools can only go so far. The government are obsessed with the system because they believe that the voting public are obsessed by league tables and testing. I disagree. As a parent and a teacher I speak to hundreds of parents who dislike the system and what it has done to schools. In a survey published in February 2009 by the National Association of Headteachers 85 per cent of the 10,000 parents asked wanted an end to SATs. The highest level of support for SATs from parents published to date was in a MORI survey of just under 1000 parents published in April 2009 in which only 44 per cent of parents supported the testing regime. Yes, parents want accountability, but they want genuine measures that encourage schools to develop in the right ways.

I would like to see a more incremental approach to pupil assessment, based on the acquisition of skills and competencies. In other words, how well does my child work in a team? How well do they communicate using a variety of media? How well does my child understand money management? What strategies does my child use to solve problems? How do they respond to difficulty? How well do they understand their own performance? The principle is the acquisition of accreditation points as pupils demonstrate usage. I would like to develop a system where every child built a portfolio of skills and competencies, each worth points that could then be measured for performance and used in comparative data. The process would of course include analysis of basic, core skills including Numeracy and Literacy, but would be far more expansive and take into account the ability to apply these skills across a vast range of applications and interests.

Our current system assumes that all children should be the same, reach the same learning states at the same age, be able to do the same things at the same time in the same way, know the same 'stuff' and share the same interests. Personalizing the system means something completely different. It seeks to develop core skills so that children then diversify and develop their own journeys. Who is it that said that all children by the age of 11 should achieve Level 4 or 5? Some children are capable far younger, some a little older. The original curriculum levels stated that Level 4 was the level of average attainment at the end of Year 6, not the pass level. I have taught children capable of taking GCSE media studies at the age of 9 and I say we should let them.

CHAPTER 9

Are they fit for the future?

Do we really give our children the best chance?

If school isn't working we can have only ourselves to blame. If our young people are leaving their formal education unable to thrive in their adult lives the system needs to look hard at itself.

Author

It is only because I have spent most of my adult life working in schools that I understand what it feels like to be a child living in one. If I, like most parents, relied on the evening feedback of my own brood I would be none the wiser. We can, of course, draw on our own memories of those 'halcyon days' and believe that things will have evolved and often hope that they have! Like religion and politics, we all have a definite view of how it should be, could be or is. Our beliefs, as with all things, are governed by our own experiences. For example, there are those who, if they can, send their children to the same school that they attended and those parents who wouldn't do so if theirs was the last school on earth. One of the most daunting things for a parent is choosing the 'right' school: what do you look for? How do you know? Above all, we all want our children's school to ensure that the routines, rules, systems, lessons and experiences work! In the next few paragraphs I hope to offer an insight into the generic experience for most children and intersperse that with some of the key issues facing our young people today.

The bell for the start of the day has just gone, a whistle has blown and children run to lines and stand, with fingers on lips, ready to file in for the start of another day. From their first day to their last, children are carefully herded and corralled through their school experience. We live in a world still haunted by the old saying 'children should be seen and not heard'. I have often read on reports and citations the phrase, 'So and so is a lovely child. He or she works silently and never make a fuss.'

One of the most common criticisms aimed at young people new to the adult workplace is that they lack initiative. They cannot solve problems for themselves and constantly need to be told what to do.

Once in the classroom, our children look at the timetable, see which lesson they are about to have, are told to fetch their exercise books, sit in their assigned places at their desks, or often on the floor, wait quietly while the teacher tells them what they will learn today. One or two children, who didn't go beforehand, will put up their hands and ask for permission to go the toilet.

Increasingly in the world of tomorrow, people will be working for themselves. They will need to set themselves targets, plan their work patterns and work unmanaged towards deadlines.

The lesson will consist of the teacher taking at least 15 minutes to explain the objective, set the context and to lead a question and answer session. In a well equipped room, this will involve the use of an interactive whiteboard, which often the teacher will monopolize. Occasionally one child will be allowed to come to the front and demonstrate something on the board. The teacher will then define what is to be done and tell the children how long they will have to complete the task.

Our young people are criticized for their inability to communicate, to generate and sustain discussion. There is a growing concern in the UK about children's decreased emotional literacy and abilities of self-expression. Yet, in my experience, the vast majority of talk in the average classroom is generated by the teacher.

The school day is punctuated for our children by breaktimes and lunchtime, during which most children are released onto the playground to run around for between ten minutes and an hour, depending on the type of break being taken. They do so come rain or shine, no matter what the temperature. The playground may be grey, an empty space. In well equipped schools, it may be decorated with some play equipment and coloured markings. The boys will tend to dominate the yard, playing soccer. The girls may perfect a dance routine or walk around, arms linked, singing or chatting. Those who aren't with the 'in crowd' just wander until the bell goes and lessons resume.

There is a growing concern that behaviour during free time and outside of school is degenerating and children appear aimless and unable to constructively amuse themselves.

At the end of the day the bell goes. Our children are set homework, often a worksheet to reinforce the lessons from earlier in the day or spellings for a test on Friday. They are armed with a reading book, chosen for them because it is the next book on the reading scheme list and they are told to read at least the next chapter so that it can be signed off. Then they stand when told, tuck their chairs under their desks and march out to their parents at the gate.

Many parents report that their children return home, either hyperactive or drained, not wanting to read or do their homework. When asked how school was, they tend to drop their bag, kick off their shoes and stomp up the stairs muttering, 'The usual, boring.'

I do not mean to be derisive or depressing, but schools are formulaic by their nature. They are obsessed by doing the right things for all the reasons explained in previous chapters; they are rules-level places. We face challenging times, driven by over-prescription, fear of behaviour and a youth that the press would have us believe is out of control. Schools are in many ways closely related to prisons; even the architecture of large school buildings with their high walls screams of internment. Schools are worlds of their own, divorced of the reality of everyday life. Routines are exactly that: inflexible, repeated day in day out.

Our children spend the vast majority of their formative waking hours in these environments. In order to understand the growing antipathy towards education from our children, we must see the world through their eyes. Schools are designed by adults, run by adults, managed by adults, monitored by adults and modified by adults. For that reason, schools have evolved little, but the blame for their failure falls often on the children and staff who exist within them.

I was fascinated by the government's Respect agenda, designed to restore order among our young people, to, among other things, reduce truancy and improve behaviour in our schools. The strategy was underpinned by introducing tougher punishments and deterrents, with blame falling squarely at the feet of parents, schools and children themselves. Of course behaviour and misbehaviour are complex issues. Many experts will cite the reasons for misbehaviour around a number of key triggers including:

- Attention
- Power
- Revenge
- Avoidance
- Boredom
- Stress

For me, most have something to do with a sense of a lack of empowerment or purpose. As adults our greatest anger stems from feelings of injustice or of powerlessness. In a rules-level world, feelings of a lack of empowerment are very common indeed. All too often students feel that education is done to them; the traditional view that the role of adults is to tell children what is right and what is wrong, what it is important to know and what it isn't.

As a result, it appears that no-one had stopped to ask how the system must change in order to improve positive feeling among the young, for education and schools. Maybe it is the system that is failing our kids, rather than our kids failing the system. The current measures are a little like giving someone with a brain tumour painkillers. It may temporarily take away the pain, but the problem is only being masked as there is no real treatment.

A number of years ago I attended a think tank group, managed by the Innovation Unit, which at the time, was part of the Department of Education. The think tank was set up to explore the issues facing schools of the future. The most enlightening inputs came from secondary pupils, invited to the day to provide consumer insight. One young man's comments struck me in particular. He asked why he was expected to learn important things first thing in the morning when, as he explained, he did his best learning in the evening. The comment for me highlighted a number of issues, one being the fact that our children are part of the 'on-demand' generation. Their lives are truly personalized. They watch what they want on TV when they want; they download and listen to the music they want to listen to when they want to listen to it. They can personalize their trainers in the colours and patterns they want. They can chat to their friends via their mobile phones and the internet when it suits them. Some schools have latched on to the online, on-demand generation through the use of internet-based learning gateways, which allow pupils and staff the opportunity to log on, research, complete, submit and track their work any time of the night and day.

Research published in 2009 based on tests carried out by Professor Russell Foster, chairman of Circadian Neuroscience at Brasenose

College, Oxford concluded that there could be biological reasons why those aged 10–20 need to sleep later and longer than the rest of us. About nine hours more, to be exact. It also suggests that students perform better in the afternoon because their body clock is programmed about two hours later, possibly for hormonal reasons. The research has led to one innovative secondary school, Monkseaton High School in North Tyneside, altering its timetable to accommodate its pupils' body clocks to ensure that learning quality is maximized.

It is crucial that the school experience is holistic and that all aspects of the school day are of equal importance. Inevitably, because of the pressures on teacher time and the vast amount of thought that goes into lessons, the times for leisure and social interaction, breaktimes, are forgotten! Why are children thrown onto the yard and told to run around, to burn off their pent-up energy? For some children this is a nightmare. It can also be boring and, at times, threatening. We must give far more thought to these times of day and fill them with stimulating opportunities for the children to develop their social and creative energies. There are some schools that are now opening their facilities to children during breaktimes; their computer suites, libraries, gyms, etc. Schools are also offering numerous activities, often run by pupils themselves; games clubs, coaching and mentoring sessions. I will explore other ideas later in the book.

Homework is an interesting and at times emotive issue. What is it actually for? Does it really add to the learning experiences for our children or are there other motives? As a parent, if my child has homework, I can keep them from under my feet while I sort out tea and other household jobs. It also gives me an idea of what they are learning at school. Often, however, 'homework sessions' end in a family row, either because it isn't being done, my child doesn't understand it, won't listen to me or, even worse, because I can't help because it's beyond my level of knowledge. Does reading a set book, which offers little interest to either child or parent, really have any productive value? Surely our children are entitled to downtime in the same way that we, as adults, are. We perceive that a day for an adult at work is harder than a day for our children at school. I would disagree; both are equally intense. After a day at work, the last thing I feel like is doing another couple of hours at home.

Of course, if we change the concept of the learning day and if all schools developed learning gateways, it would be impossible to differentiate between homework and school. It would be bound in the same, interactive, research-based journey of discovery.

Many schools have in recent years set up school councils and explored the development of pupil voice. However, mostly pupil involvement in school management and development is kept well within the comfort zone. The danger attached to genuinely developing pupil voice is that pupils will not always come up with things you want to hear. They are, as we all know, brutally honest and often highly challenging. If we allow pupils a voice we must also act on their opinions, otherwise the children quickly realize that their involvement is no more than superficial.

What I have come to realize, in my years in education, is that given the opportunity and the right guidance, children are extremely observant and innovative. Their suggestions are rarely censored by experience in the same ways ours are and, therefore, they are often really creative and exciting.

We should be asking our school councils how we can improve writing in our schools, playground behaviour and attendance, in the same way that large companies spend fortunes on market research.

We must find ways to increase opportunities for our children to be genuinely independent and self-selective. We must give them room to make decisions and, at times, room to live with the consequences so that they can learn from their mistakes and choices. If we wrap children too tightly in cotton wool, we will suffocate them and they will never be able to face the challenges of the world around them.

We must respect our children's opinions, identities and choices and be flexible enough to work to them, rather than ploughing on regardless, imposing more rules and routines in order to smother their individuality.

How often do we hear the criticism that our children cannot take responsibility for their actions? Sadly at the moment our system doesn't allow them the opportunity to do so.

CHAPTER 10

Making school magical!

How to make school the next must-have

Where we are can govern how we feel; our confidence, sense of belonging, wellbeing and value. Our children must be able to spend their days in environments that comfort and inspire them, spaces designed for them and, to an extent, by them.

Author

If, as I expressed earlier, the curriculum in schools is about every minute and experience our children have in school, we must spend some time looking at our children's physical environment. As we have learned more and more about how our brains function and how our thoughts are stimulated, we have been able to understand the concepts of environment beyond the aesthetic and it has developed into a science.

If we are to explore the issues facing our schools thoroughly we must begin to examine our children's holistic experience of the place in which they spend the vast majority of their waking hours.

As I travel around the world visiting schools, I constantly marvel at the conditions in which we expect our children to thrive. Education should be seen as a journey of discovery. It should spark the flames of imagination and light the fires of curiosity and development. Children are the most precious gifts bestowed on any of us and should be nurtured and valued above all things. Our schools should be exciting hubs of energy, life and wonder, but many are not.

The majority of our schools are highly functional, institutionalized spaces. Those built after the last war are clasp-built, prefabricated monstrosities, already rotting and corroding. Pre-war schools, many of which are Victorian, are sad shells, attacked by the ravages of time.

No matter when they were built, our schools all possess disturbingly similar architecture; a series of classrooms laid out with wooden or plastic furniture, display boards ravaged by the drawing pins of time, lifeless linoleum floors, a hall, where children are made to sit for assembly, usually on the floor, stained with generations of lunch and chip fat, and a playground with hard, pitted surfaces, smoothed only by the generations that have frozen there before.

Of course, the routines defined in the previous chapter serve only to reinforce the penal image. The high, caged fencing that now encases our schools, to keep us in and them out, finishes the picture.

In 1997 the new Labour government in the UK placed investment in schools and, particularly, school buildings, at the very top of their manifesto. That investment has indeed been forthcoming, mainly in our secondary schools. The schools that have been through one of the rebuild or refurbishment programmes look stunning and some have highly innovative design features that include high, airy central atriums that serve as meeting places and focal points. Some have developed under a human scaling model that allows vast schools to feel more personal by creating schools within schools. There are strides forward but we must be very careful.

Even with the new initiatives, schools are not being designed for the future. Yes, they are gleaming glass and chrome structures which raise morale in the short term, but there is little thought for the fitness for future purpose. They are still built using the blueprint of yesterday's school systems. I have spoken to so many frustrated headteachers of 'new build' schools, who despair at the lack of creativity and real design freedom allowed in the architectural process, not through a lack of effort but because, when schools and local people have come up with what they want, they have been told that classrooms need to be of set dimensions, designed in certain ways and used for set purposes. One of the most fundamental issues is that of perception: a school of the future is not a building, it cannot start with a structural blueprint that, once built and inhabited, will define what happens within the space. A school of the future is about understanding the learning and management of that learning; it is about creating flexible, almost liquid, environments that can change and develop as quickly as the world around them. In other words, we must design the process before we build the tools and this is a massive cultural shift in educational thinking. Think of interactive whiteboards; we brought in the tool and then worked out how to use it. We need to work out what we want and then create the space to house it. More than anything, however, the critical question is one of ownership and actually it doesn't much matter about the space if the children feel that they have a real sense of ownership and empowerment and that they can inhabit the space, rather than feel that they visit it but that it belongs to the adults.

Old or new, the problems remain the same, as with the curriculum. There is a one size fits all, prescriptive outlook, that assumes that the 'System' knows best.

There has also been little focus on looking beyond education, to see what can be learnt from private business and industry about the development of buildings, interiors and atmosphere. Major companies are investing massive amounts of money in the design, decoration and furnishing of their buildings – for some it has become a science. There is a growing realization that productivity is directly linked to environment. Of course in the public sector money is an issue, but there is a balance to be had between prudence and luxury. When we decorate, furnish, renovate or build our schools, how much thought and time is given to the science and psychology of environment? How much time and thought is given to ownership of space?

I want to stay here and be part of this

Over the last few years, I have been fortunate enough to work with two hugely successful organizations and to be invited to visit their headquarters. They both share a great deal in common; a commitment to the future and young people and to the welfare and wellbeing of their staff. Both organizations have got it stunningly right in my mind. Both organizations have so much we could learn from about how we design and manage the physical environments of our schools.

The first is Microsoft UK. I was stunned by the thought and creativity spent on the design of the environment. Within seconds of arriving, I felt valued, special; I wanted to stay and be part of it forever. Isn't that what our kids should feel when they walk into their schools? The place was full of light, it was colourful, unsurprisingly, bristling with technology, but nurturing and hugely welcoming. It was explained to me that each area had been furnished and decorated with shapes and colours that stimulate the right brain functions for the tasks completed in those spaces. Many spaces were large and flexible. A great deal of thought had gone into the leisure areas, which contained computer games consoles, soft furnishings, plants, plasma screens and stimulating artwork, and as for the main cafeteria . . . well! It is no wonder that Microsoft is consistently voted one of the best places in the UK to work, year on year.

The second is an organization I hold in very high regard. They, too, are committed to their community and to their people. EGG was one of the world's first internet banks, with a global reputation for innovation and customer care. Outside of education, I have never wanted to work anywhere as much, and why? Because of the atmosphere and buzz of the place; it too is a riot of design and colour. It is light, airy and flexible in its layout. As you walk through the doors, you are greeted by music, unobtrusive but current, cool and hip. On the walls are light sculptures and clever softening lights. The main atrium has, at its centre, a coffee shop surrounded by discreet meeting areas. The main hub of the place, a huge call centre, is surprisingly calm. Areas are zoned. Projected on to the walls are MTV and Sky Sports News. The main training room resembles the starship *Enterprise* and the core meeting room looks like a New York loft apartment. Around the main call centre halls are 'break-out' rooms, containing computer games, pool tables, drinks facilities and TVs and there is even a massage room. The place is draped in banners celebrating staff and previous achievements and depicting snapshots of the company's history. I was fascinated when the thinking behind the company ethos was explained to me; it is a young company, both in terms of trading years and in terms of employee profile. The key business of banking does not have an outwardly glamorous profile and call centre work can be high pressured. The company was aware of this and set about consulting their staff to find ways in which the environment could redress the balance and underline the ethos. The results are stunning. It changed my thinking as a school leader.

EGG and Microsoft both realize that an organization belongs to its people and it is vital that the physical fabric of that organization promotes that sense of ownership and purpose. It should evoke the culture of its people and promote the key drivers for the business' success. Both have worked closely with their employees to develop the environment and achieve the stunning facilities they have. I am interested in the resonance between both companies' employees and the children we educate. This is not really surprising, I suppose, given that both organizations are 'new technology' providers and that the employee profile is young and dynamic.

How can our system get it so wrong by comparison? They are places of 'learning' that are often divorced from the outside world. Our children must go there; they have no choice, it is the law. Why should schools not have computer game systems for breaktimes, groovy break-out areas, current music cascading out in welcome, soft furnishings, light, flexible spaces and modern art and design?

Ownership is at the heart of the issue. We need to be very clear who our schools belong to. They do not belong to you or me; they belong to the generation of children who inhabit them. It therefore follows that children must feel the spaces and environments that surround them demonstrate and support that sense of ownership.

There are significant numbers of adults who, when they become parents of school age children, relive much of their own education experience. I know many parents who, as a result of bad experiences, have become 'school phobic'. They feel deeply uncomfortable in school buildings, the structures, the layouts, the smells. For many children, both now and then, schools were institutional structures, largely alien places, owned squarely by the adults who inhabit them. I remember one of my teachers, who was definitely from the old school, had his classroom set up in reverence to the ancient gods. He was a terrifying man; he was also a pipe smoker. Whenever we did something wrong, which was frequently in my case, he would make us bow down before a poster of Poseidon and beg forgiveness. He would then stand over us, barking instructions, as we did so. The classroom was his kingdom and we were privileged visitors. In terms of progress, it was the poorest year I had in school. Clearly the vast majority of classrooms today don't replicate this experience, particularly the aroma of stale tobacco, however many are managed by staff who consider their own routines and comforts first.

The school building and the warmth of it and the way we are allowed to interact with it, make a huge difference to the way that we, as children, develop within it.

If you attended a school concert and, on arriving at the school hall, were told to sit on the floor, you would be extremely unhappy, particularly if some staff and governors were sitting on chairs. It would feel disrespectful, humiliating, indeed, just plain wrong. This, however, is what we do to children, yet we expect them to love us and our building.

As teachers, we set up our classrooms the way we like them and impose the layout on our children. We choose the colour of the backing paper on the walls, we decide who sits where. Emotional safety and security are often linked to a sense of ownership and belonging. Therefore, to help develop these states of mind in a school we must give children a feeling that the environment they inhabit is theirs.

I have seen some stunning classrooms over time; classrooms laid out and developed by teachers and children in partnership. As a result, these classrooms have tables and chairs set out to ensure the best visual access to the board, to the teacher, to the resources, but the rooms also contain lounge areas, highly decorated break-out zones, areas filled with interactive puzzles and games, posters of the pupils' icons, areas with CD players linked to headphones, together with a selection of pupils' favourite music. The walls are brightly coloured and adorned with examples of work and art chosen by the kids, the layouts of the displays designed in partnership. Also on the walls are affirmation posters selected and designed by children, expressing old chestnuts like 'There's no I in TEAM' and 'Today I am going to do something amazing'. Many who read this will have had similar experiences of these kinds of fantastic learning space, mostly, I would guess, in primary school classrooms. Surely all learning spaces should feel as homely and as accommodating? All schools for children of all ages!

There has been some interesting work over recent years in many secondary schools, which have been researching the concepts of human scaling. Many have had funding help from The Gulbenkian Foundation, which have produced some very interesting case studies. The clear thinking behind the work was that many schools are vast and impersonal places, particularly schools for our older children and that the sheer scale and anonymity made real individual development and growth difficult. The schools that have engaged in this work have thought strategically to redesign their internal and external spaces in order to create environments that are welcoming, less daunting, personal and stimulating. The work has resulted in remodelling, not only of spaces and classrooms but how whole schools are structured and run, proving hugely significant. The key message, though, is that an investment in the learning spaces is vital and not age-determinant. After all if it was just for children under 11, why have Microsoft and EGG gone to such great expense?

As schools we may not have the money currently to reinvent the fabric of our buildings or invest in the kind of interior design demonstrated by big business, but we can work together on many of the key principles of spaces that promote belonging, that are not uniformly the same, that internally do not resemble prisons and that are designed around the people that inhabit them. We can, if we are in a community lucky enough to be designated a new school building, be in a position to turn to the commissioned architect and ask key questions like: what have you done to ensure that the layout inspires our children? How have you ensured that it is fit for future purpose and do you know about the Microsoft and EGG campuses?

The most critical issue, however, is that local authorities, government agencies, schools and governing boards must prepare carefully for the challenge of future school design by understanding the function of future schools and the activities that these buildings may house in the future. Above all, they must ensure that all learning environments are designed for and by the end users; our children. There would be huge value in educators talking to design architects around the world who spend their lives designing spaces that attract and captivate our young in shopping malls and high streets.

CHAPTER 11

Breaking down the walls

Educating with the community

The truth is we are all responsible for our children's education because it does not happen exclusively between the hours of nine and three, five days a week. Everything from an internet search to a new smell can spell the beginning of a major learning moment.

Author

Schools are fascinating places; they seem to have invisible force fields that prevent non-teaching adults from crossing the threshold. They seem to hold a mystique for people outside of the profession. It occurs to me that belonging to a school must be a little like being a freemason. You tend not to talk about it in public, the vast majority feel a little intimidated by you and there is often a high level of mistrust.

One of the great misinformed beliefs is that education is for schools and managed by teachers and the rest of us perform other roles in life.

I have to say that a great deal of myth and misunderstanding surround schools. Sometimes, I must confess, the schools themselves feel secure promoting those myths. However, for the good of our children we must break them down.

I have heard colleagues say to me, 'Our school would be fine if it wasn't for the parents.' I have seen headteachers actively discourage parental involvement. The invisible force fields are erected, often due to the misconception that schools are the place for learning and that the world beyond is for doing, once you have learnt. I am sure that many of you remember the disparaging saying that, 'Those who can, do. Those who can't, teach.'

We live in a world obsessed by classifying and pigeon-holing and, as a result, educational opportunities for our children are grossly underexploited. Schools should be seen as the meeting places of experiences that then become the centres of learning. Learning is at its best when it is drawn from the communities surrounding the school. The school's job should then be to help the community and the children make sense of those experiences and to help draw out the learning opportunities.

Education remains one of the highest priorities for us all. Not surprisingly, it becomes the number one priority once you are a parent. Annual surveys produced by Phi Delta Kappa and Gallop consistently place education as the most important public issue for about 50 per cent of parents; higher than health care, social security and even the economy. For non-parents this falls to around one-third, but it still comes in the top two or three of important public issues.

For most parents the times that they enter the school premises and cross the invisible force field are for stage-managed events: parents' evenings, concerts, sports days. Sometimes parents with the time and the inclination will come into school to offer time and will end up hearing readers or possibly knitting. I know that often parents feel inadequate when education is discussed in relation to their children, Maybe it has something to do with the experience we all had as children and the fact that, at the time, we saw teachers as greater, wiser, untouchable beings. Maybe it has something to do with the unsettling experience we all have at some stage of our children's school careers, when they are working with a teacher that they idolize; 'Oh, Mum, Mr Bloggs is so funny.' 'Mrs Jones says that we don't do it that way.', 'Mrs Smith is amazing. I can tell the time now; she explained it so that I understood it.' Moments like this make us all wince, they make us feel somehow like lesser beings, particularly if we have just spent the entire weekend trying to explain to our child that the big hand tells us the hours and the little hand shows us the minutes.

We, as teachers, are trained to communicate, explain and translate, but it is parents who can provide the substance. It would be very interesting to audit the different jobs, interests and experiences of the parents that make up our school communities. My guess is that they will be diverse: plumbers, lawyers, builders, salespeople, doctors, entertainers, model-makers, painters, sports fanatics, mechanics, share dealers . . . Imagine the power of pooling their knowledge, experience and skill and encouraging them to work with teachers to design learning experiences for our children, in partnership. We could create a whole universe of opportunity. These opportunities exist now, in all of our communities. All it would take would be for our schools to run a skills and interests audit among their parents. Listening to children read can be useful, but parents are a hugely important resource to schools and education and they are underexploited and underestimated, both by educators and parents themselves. Later in the book I will share examples of how parents and teachers can work together to create extraordinary learning opportunities.

If we get the process right and develop true partnership, we would not, as parents, ask at parents' evenings: 'What are you teaching my child this year?' but 'What are *we* teaching my child this year?'

Creating music together is an activity that
encourages good communication within a class

Education can only be truly effective if we break down the 'us and them' culture. To do this successfully we cannot rely on one or the other to change the ethos, we must work in partnership. One of the most common criticisms levelled at schools is their poor communication with parents. The criticism is often made by passive parents who want information 'delivered'. It is often levelled by parents who perceive the education of their children to be the preserve of the school. Education is bigger than that. It can rise or fall on the strength of the partnership and it can be limited by the commitment of one or other party. To that end, we must not see schools as the places where children learn, but the places where children can make sense of their learning. If learning is controlled solely by teachers and schools the learning will always be divorced from reality. It is parents who often are the bridge to providing the context for learning; their experiences and skills are vital if we are to develop an approach fit for the future.

We must similarly transform the understanding of the relationship between private and public sector, between business and education. For generations we have lived with a 'moral wall' separating the two. Education has for too long exposed its vocational roots by seeing business and industry as for capital gain: 'As teachers we care for people, as industrialists you care for profit' and, as a result, never the twain shall meet. Business and industry often see the public sector, and particularly education, as a beggar with a bowl: 'What you want is our money; where is the benefit? A piece about donation in the local paper is nice, but shortlived and of no real value.' As schools, we make the mistake of believing that money is what the private sector is good for and the only way that they can prove their philanthropy. As a result, no genuine relationships are made.

In truth we are in the same business; securing our futures. Education seeks to develop the adult citizens who will improve the world in which we live. Business needs well-educated citizens to ensure businesses and industry thrive in the future. It is, after all, our children's generation who will fund our pensions!

Forward-thinking businesses understand this and are already doing a significant amount of work with local schools to share skills and thinking, thanks in part to the development of what business calls CSR – Corporate Social Responsibility. However, it is still not common practice and is particularly rare in primary/elementary school settings. We must work harder to make the links, to use the expertise of our local communities and the businesses within them to develop the educational experiences of our children. Each community has on its door step businesses small and large which carry equal weight in the impact they can have. The experience of a local shop owner, talking with children about stock control, pricing and shop layout, has equal significance to the multinational sharing thinking about marketing campaigns. The local beauty salon working with children on how to become hairdressers or beauticians has as much resonance as the big-time soccer coach talking about a career in football.

Some may say that we do this already through work experience programmes and through the new diploma system launched in England in 2008. This is not enough and it happens far too late in our children's schooling. If we are to add value to the skills and competencies we are teaching in schools, we must help children see how they can be translated into practice in later life. This needs to happen as soon as children begin their formal education. Our children love pretending to be pilots, hairdressers, soldiers and sports stars. As young children they play at it for hours. They are already trying to make sense of the world around them. In partnership, we can harness this play and help our children take it to the next level: a game can become an ambition, an ambition can become tangible, but only if we provide the learning, skills and contexts in partnership. If you like, we as teachers have the pen and paper, the wider community can provide the story. If the story comes solely from teachers it will always feel make-believe; if it comes from all of us it can be real.

As communities we have enormous worth. Together we must bring down the force fields, open up our thinking, overcome our prejudices and develop education together.

Jude Kelly, the inspirational Artistic Director of the South Bank Centre in London, recently observed that as adults we rarely have anything to do with children who aren't our own; we see them as other people's 'responsibility'. She is right, yet they represent all of our futures. If, in your old age, you need the help of the medical profession, the likelihood is that the people who treat you will be the generation of young people we see before us today. It starts to make you view our children slightly differently. Ultimately we need a paradigm shift that will see us all take responsibility for our children's learning and education. When I say 'our children', I mean it in a broad sense, not just the ones we parent. Jude has herself set an example by working with local schools and the South Bank Centre to provide a different learning experience for children in London. Instead of going to their school the young people went to the South Bank Centre for half a term, doing all of their learning through the work of the Centre. It was a fantastic success. While it is true we don't all have a South Bank Centre at our disposal, we can all help to provide richer, more meaningful experiences for our youth. If education is about stimulating the development of aspiration and of values in our children, if it is about helping them connect with and find a sense of purpose in their communities, then as communities we must all work to make this happen.

CHAPTER 12

The way forward

Summarizing Section 1 and setting up Section 2

The crisis surrounding education is as stark as any we face today. The need for action, for transformation, is as urgent as dealing with the declining environment or the global economy. Our children are growing fast; their need is now!

Author

In this final chapter of Section 1, I want to summarize the issues that face our education system as we head into the challenges our children face in their futures.

There is wide recognition around the world that the traditional models of schooling are no longer fit for purpose; in many countries government departments are investing heavily in exploring the future and the changes that the system will need to make to truly face up to and meet the challenge. At present, however, governments are not brave enough to understand that the future is not a continued number of reforms, tweaks and new policies. It is about radical transformation which requires two critical questions to define it: first, what kind of future are we preparing our children for? And second, what do we need our children to be like – as human beings, citizens, individuals – if they are going to be able to cope with the challenges of that future? We cannot allow our policy makers to continue to develop education in the short-term reactive way they have been over the last 20 years or so. We have had a succession of disastrous initiatives and policies that now litter the floors of classrooms around the world and that have largely had a detrimental impact on our schools and our pupils. In the United States the clumsy 'No Child Left Behind' strategy that defined George W. Bush's educational vision was obsessed with narrow outcomes, not real development. We have had similar in the UK where even well-meaning and pupil-centric sentiments such as 'Personalized Learning' have been scrapped because nobody could truly define what it meant or how it could be done. This was partly because, like most educational strategic development, it had to be tagged on to existing policies and approaches which has resulted in confusion and lack of foundation.

The stakes are unbelievably high. Our kids only get the one chance; we cannot therefore afford to get it wrong. How could we, 20 years from now, apologise to a failed generation? It is not as though they will get that time again.

Partly the problems that face us are political. Numerous commissioned reports and world-renowned experts have set out the challenge and the scale of the issues we face. Unfortunately, many of the crucial messages are uncomfortable and politically dangerous. The reason is that we are not talking about gentle evolution or mild development. We are talking about that need for wholesale system transformation. In the UK our education system is dominated by central, civil-servant control, a fact envied by many in larger, state-governed nations like America and Australia. The truth, though, is that this approach relies on visionary people who have constant exposure to, and experience of, the challenges that face our children, our teachers and our schools. This is simply not the case among the majority of civil servants who, at best, are trying to please too many people with too many different agendas. Having spoken to and worked with a number of politicians from varying political backgrounds around the world, it appears that many are limited by the ability and vision of their civil servant teams, where there are too many capable managers and not enough visionary leaders.

What is really very sad and of great concern is that, to minimize disruption and dissent, government departments with a remit for education have, in many countries across the free world, actively undermined educational expertise, thinking and challenge in order to ensure central control of what should be a local, even personal, issue.

Professor Sir Ken Robinson, says of the system in his seminal book *Out of Our Minds*:

> Raising academic standards alone will not solve the problems we face: it may compound them. To move forward we need a fresh understanding of intelligence, of human capacity and of the

nature of creativity. Human intelligence is richer and more dynamic than we have been led to believe by formal academic education. Advances in the scientific studies of the brain are confirming that human intelligence is complex and multifaceted. We can think about the world and our experiences in terms of sight, in touch, in sound, in movement and in many other ways. This is why the world is full of music, dance, architecture, design, practical technology, relationships and values. Brain-scanning techniques show that even simple actions draw simultaneously on different functions and regions of the brain.

Human culture is as rich and diverse as it is because human intelligence is so complex and dynamic. We all have great natural capacities, but we all have them differently. There are not only two types of people, academic or non academic. We all have distinctive profiles of intellectual abilities with different strengths in visual intelligences, in sound, in movement, in mathematical thinking and the rest. Academic education looks only for certain sorts of ability. Those who have it often have other abilities that are ignored: those who don't are likely to be seen as not intelligent at all. Highly able people are turned away from companies or lost in them because their education tells the wrong story. If we're serious about developing human resources, the first step is to recognize how diverse and individual those resources are.

(Ken Robinson, Out of Our Minds, *pages 9–10)*

The problem has become global. High-profile businesses and business icons are so concerned that they have started to invest massive amounts of personal resource into driving forward the agenda. Bill Gates is a striking example, saying in his keynote address to the Government Leaders Forum in Washington, D. C. in March 2009 that, 'Education is an essential foundation that we cannot skip or neglect if we hope to provide sustainable, long-term economic and entre-preneurial growth.'

Yet governments still find themselves trapped by our fixation on the past. I guess that education and academia have been bound together for so many generations that they have become fused. In the UK there have been attempts by the government to recognize the process. The Innovation Unit was set up to explore future systems and methodologies until it was privatized due to a cut in funding in 2007. Think tanks such as DEMOS and Futurelab have provided a number of future sight scenarios. England's curriculum authority, the QCA, under the guidance of its former dynamic Director of Curriculum Mick

Waters, have been developing blueprints for exciting future approaches to schooling. In China the government have been embarking on the largest education systems transformation agenda ever seen. Some of the work has been good, very good, but most changes have been seen as marginal and many have never really been given the momentum, funding or support to fulfil their potential. Most importantly, despite the billions spent, very little has really changed.

Why now? The system has functioned largely untouched for over one hundred years but, as with so much of the world we live in, our rate of progress and understanding about the brain, child development and education have accelerated beyond all comprehension since the end of the last war. Sadly, the system has not kept pace. We are a little like a medical profession that, regardless of knowing about the great cures and procedures that have evolved over time, is still using the cures of the Tudor age.

As in so many Western cultures, we are conservative by nature. We are a breed that finds comfort in the familiar and threat in the unknown. Occasionally, though, a generation comes along that has the courage to take strides forward for the betterment of humanity. I feel passionately that for education that time is now and we must be the generation. If we don't take up the challenge the consequences could be catastrophic.

The current apathy towards education was not created by the current generation of children, but by our generation. Whether we admit it or not, most of us know that the system that we went through may have delivered results, but it didn't deliver us a future. At the time of writing this book, the latest exam results have been published for our 18-year-old school leavers and I am proud, as an educator, that yet again our youngsters have broken all previous records and that success and pass rates are at an all-time high. This, of course, sparks off the traditional debate that exams must be easier; they were tougher in our day, and so on. I simply refuse to believe that this is true. I work with children every single day and I know that the generations of youngsters I work with are more capable than they have ever been. As I have already discussed, they are capable of handling and processing information on a greater scale and at faster rates, they have access to information streams and experiences that aid the acceleration of their development. They may not be as grammatically sure-footed as previous generations but they have no need to be. Communication has changed and they are not called upon to exercise those skills as frequently as we were, but then we cannot manipulate technology in the way that they can. It is not a better or worse state, it is just different.

I do believe, however, that the exam system has been devalued because it is becoming less and less relevant in its current format and it is for that reason that our youngsters are struggling to develop careers despite their exam success. They are doing everything that is asked of them; it is what we are asking of them that is wrong.

For system transformation to take hold we must look within, change the balance of power and move our view of education forward. It must become less political and the mistrust between educationalists and politicians must go. We must get over our fixation with academic standards and high stakes testing and stop believing that increased academic rigour is the answer to our future needs.

It is interesting that, as the education system has become more academically focused in the West, the East has overtaken our productivity and industrial success, during which time they have looked to diversify and explore alternative methodologies of schooling. In places such as Hong Kong and Singapore they are spending vast amounts of money and time developing highly creative and dynamic approaches to future learning. In Europe, too, there are some exciting and innovative strides being made in education, with excellent results, particularly in Finland, where personal development and skills are at the heart of educational development. In Australia, Canada and New Zealand, too, there has been a growing emphasis on the development of children's behaviours, skills and emotional wellbeing. In all of these cases children are tested significantly less than our own children. There is far greater trust in teachers and teaching and a marked decrease in central political intervention. All of these countries perform considerably better than the UK according to the PISA international rankings for reading and writing ability among 15 year olds, last published in late 2006. Interestingly, when the 2003 tables by PISA were published the Japanese reacted with shock, finding themselves nowhere near the top-performing nations. As a result they replaced what they saw as a 'soft' education system with a high pressure one; this had little impact when the 2006 figures were published. There is a stark message here for governments and systems like the UK's and America's which place high-stakes testing at the core of policy.

Our children need to develop their self-confidence, self-worth, creative and innovative thinking, team-working and communication skills, to have a chance of competing in the global market place. We are all aware of this, nationally and internationally, but when was the last time your children had a lesson that focused on these skills as a priority? Where in the testing system are these skills assessed?

It would be unfair, however, to focus all of the blame and pressure on politics and politicians, because the truth is that the opportunities already exist; schools have the power to innovate and to transform their learning approaches. Recent government-sponsored reports on future curriculum development such as the Rose Review are pointing the way to greater flexibility and autonomy and that is a great reason for optimism. It does, however, lay down a real challenge to the education community and society in general. In some ways the safety net of being able to say, 'Wouldn't it be great if . . . but of course we can't because we aren't allowed' has been removed and that has meant that the onus is on us to make it happen. We have listened to the rallying cries of gurus such as Sir Ken Robinson, Lord Putnam, Mick Waters, Sir John Jones and Ted Wragg for years now and the truth is that we must stop waiting for someone else to give us the answer or to explicitly give us permission. It is time to spread our own wings and fly. This is an easy sentiment, as to do this is a challenge all of its own that requires great courage, vision, leadership, commitment and skill. It is time for the education profession to stand up and prove its professional status, it is time for communities to pull together and create a powerful vision for education and then to play active roles in making it happen.

In Section 2 I will explore some possible methodologies and approaches that schools can apply now in order to help them evolve and meet the challenges we face. Many are based on strategies that we developed in my time at Grange and that have been proven in practice. It is to an extent their story, the story of a group of amazing staff, courageous governors, trusting parents and, above all, miraculous children. I will also address the challenges of leading change in our schools.

The future is bright; the education system is filled with stunning creativity, dynamic leaders and future thinkers ready to drive our systems forward. By working in partnership with parents, we can evolve an approach that is not just fit for purpose, but is about LIVING, LEARNING and LAUGHING for every one of our children.

SECTION 2

The way it could be

CHAPTER 13

Creating the vision

The thinking behind the 'Grange way'

At what point did you stop dreaming about who you could become or what you may be? At what point did what you are become the limit of your ambitions? We can be whatever our vision allows us.

Author

Grange Primary School

Since the first National Curriculum was introduced in the UK at the beginning of the 1990s, there have been nearly 700 new government initiatives and directives within the education system. There have also been some extraordinary new ideas and understandings developed and published about the way we learn and the challenges facing us. As a result, I, like so many educators, found myself confused, stressed and unclear of what we should be doing and how. For me, clarity arrived when I decided that implementing systems, no matter how exciting or how legally binding, was not the way to improve our school for our children and that the answer lay in the children themselves.

I took over Grange Primary School in the last part of the academic year of 2001/02. The school was typical of so many struggling in the system we inhabit today; the staff were stressed, morale was low and the school was struggling to define its identity and purpose. As a result, the educational experience for the children was disconnected and irrelevant.

The staff at Grange were committed and vastly experienced professionals, dedicated to the school and, most importantly, to its children. They had, however, lost their focus. Teachers were delivering a set curriculum by the book, as prescribed by successive government directives and strategies. They were doing so to ensure they were doing what they were told to. Exam results were poor and, as a result, the local authority was pressuring the school to intensify its efforts and focus on test preparation and improvement. This led to greater drops in morale and a declining holistic purpose. In turn, this had accelerated the school's spiral of decline. Teachers knew that they were not providing a vibrant experience for the children and the children could see no purpose to their learning. In truth the school had reached a point of serious disenfranchisement. Staff were not teaching with passion and the children were learning with even less.

One of the most cataclysmic strategies employed by people in charge of school improvement over the last 15 years has been the misunderstanding that to raise standards, schools must concentrate on systems, delivering more of them and more intensively. Of course, when approaches like this are deployed, children as individuals become lost in the numbers game; they become statistics. I took a break from working in schools because I found myself seeing my children as percentage points in examination outcomes. 'Jonny isn't going to get level 4. He's at least 15 marks away, so that means a 2 per cent drop in the figures. Who can I work on to get a level 4 to balance the books? Oh I know, Elsie. She is only two or three marks away from level 4, I'll concentrate on her. That way I can ensure that our results hit the targets we were set for this year.'

Refreshed and starting anew at Grange, we began by going right back to basics. It meant looking at our children and asking ourselves what kind of people we wanted them to be at the end of their journey at Grange. It was time for the school to look again deep into its heart and rediscover its moral imperative. In my opinion it is vital that any school looking to embark on a transformation agenda must start at the core, the foundations, of its approach, otherwise we end up in a universe of initiatives orbiting like satellites around an already overloaded system. School leaders must find the courage to give the school community time; to resist the pressures of outside agencies to deliver within tight timescales.

True transformation cannot be rushed and must be borne from clarity of vision that becomes a passion so strong that it drives the school and its community through the tough journeys to come.

It is an approach that I can best describe as a distillation of ideas. It is a process I have seen in many successful schools and other organizations and it must start with the development of a truly honest and trusting culture. This, of course, can be tough when you realize that in many of our struggling schools there are some exhausted, and sometimes damaged, staff who are existing on virtually no self-esteem and whose passion has long since evaporated. In so many schools there is such a culture of pressure for progress that there is a danger that we try to implement sweeping reform too quickly which often leaves many staff behind, confused, scared and angry. The success at Grange was built on a different paradigm; one which was built on conversations, conversations that became increasingly honest and routed in professional instinct and wider communication. I have long been concerned that we save our best leadership skills for when we engage with the children and forget many when we deal with our adult community. For example, we identify the different needs of individual pupils so that we can meet those needs and so encourage progress but we don't look at the needs of individual members of staff in the same way.

It is equally important that we don't obsess with knowing what the final structures and models will look like before we begin the process of transformation. I have seen the same mistakes made so often: people want the answers to all the questions before you begin and, in so many ways, that will instantly defeat the culture of innovation and creativity needed to achieve something amazing.

So, at Grange, we began our process of distillation by:

The asking of abstract questions

For example:

How do we turn our school into Disneyland ?
What would I want to learn if I was 8 years old?
How do we sell learning to the children?
Why are Literacy and Numeracy boring?

What is interesting and very exciting is that people respond with enthusiasm and thought because, all of a sudden, the questions are not loaded, they do not have predesigned answers. There is no right or wrong, which immediately takes so much of the pressure off. Each question at Grange would spark another and another. One of my happiest moments in the early days came when I walked in to the staff room one lunchtime to find the place alive with debate about one of the abstract questions we had thrown in at the staff meeting the night before. It was clear that just by asking questions and provoking debate we had managed to start a process that was leading to greater communication, a growing sense of empowerment and real optimism.

It wasn't long before the second stage of the distillation process had begun to evolve:

The generation of ideas and the start of action research

Staff would find that they had common thoughts or ideas and they would start to develop new relationships with people working in different areas of the school. Sometimes this would happen with people who had worked together before, but on a very superficial level, as there had been a perception that they didn't have a lot in common, that they were different types of teachers. The role of the leadership team was to encourage the development of ideas and see people trial some of their suggestions, beginning a process of action research. What is particularly positive about this is that reticent staff don't hold people back but the invitation is there for all to participate in. Also, it doesn't rely on that stultifying strategy dependent on complete consensus.

Interestingly, more and more people developed into the culture really quickly meaning that the school had developed a momentum that could be used to take the development further. This then evolved into the third stage of distillation:

The sharing of ideas and honest conversations

In many ways this becomes the most difficult stage, as honesty and time are crucial. It is a time when the staff must draw together, celebrate and review their action research, process and progress. What is critical is that staff are honest and generous in their input, sharing both what has worked and what hasn't. It is also vital that staff don't stop at the superficial level but explore why there have been positive or negative outcomes. This leads to a whole new layer of conversation where people share thinking that sparks new ideas and collaborations. This momentum can be harnessed by the leadership team, who must start to take ideas and develop possible strategies which can lead to the design of whole-school approaches.

The development and design of whole school strategies

What follows is then the ability to marry ideas, projects and thinking into whole-school strategies that can then begin to help redesigning practice and can be evolved into systems. The process at no stage feels like a top-down model of development or implementation which therefore reduces the level of possible conflict and increases buy in. At Grange it resulted in a notional five-year development plan being completed in 18 months.

What was clear from the early conversations we had was that we wanted to define our children by their personalities, their skills, their competencies and value, not by the levels they achieved in their tests. I have heard so many teachers say things like, 'Sammy? Oh yes, great kid, level 5 for sure!' What does that tell us about Sammy or why she is a great kid? We wanted to be able to show prospective parents around Grange and, when introducing any of them to our eldest children, say, 'If you bring your child to our school, this is the kind of person they will become.' It was clear to us that to improve our children's education we must first improve their self-esteem and self-worth. So many children who were failing, or who had failed, within our system had done so because they lacked confidence, self-esteem and personal purpose. Most of those children are labelled as 'special needs' and given a diet of more simple work in the hope that they would miraculously make up ground and become 'okay'.

Our conversations really began when we set about developing what we called a 'Learning Profiles Policy'. We started by looking at the children currently in our highest year group, our 10 and 11 year olds. We wanted to identify what our 'successful' children looked like, how they behaved in different situations, how they handled challenges, problems, interactions with other people, information and technology. We also wanted to identify, in direct contrast, what behaviours our least successful children exhibited. This process helped us to clarify the kind of behaviours we wanted to actively develop among our pupils. By creating a profile for a successful learner at the end of their journey at Grange, we could then break that profile down and build a strategy to actively develop that profile from the time children arrived at Grange, through our nursery facility at 3 years old. We then created a policy that defined what kind of behaviours would need to be developed each year for the children to evolve as learners. The policy was built around the following key questions:

What learning strategies we are promoting this year?
What opportunities we will provide for developing independence?
What key study skills we are developing this year?
How we will communicate these targets to the children?
How we are going to measure the success?
How we will celebrate the successes with the children?

The process made explicit for the first time what was central to our philosophy; that we at Grange were going to concentrate on developing human beings. By creating a new purpose we were able to start to make sense of the curriculum, the new initiatives and the new thinking surrounding child development, because every time we examined an external strategy we were able to ask how it would support the development of our children's learning profiles. Although the policy was quite rough and has since been replaced, it wasn't so much the final document that was important but the process we went through, the conversations, the development of new relationships and of constructive thinking, that was profound.

The next significant stage in our development was to explore how to deliver a curriculum and to design learning experiences which maintained the integrity of the crucial core skills our children needed – reading, writing, numeracy – while creating a vibrant learning experience that the children felt was not only important to them now, but also in the future. We needed to develop a highly creative approach to overcome the system overload that had blighted Grange for so long. How were we going to create a learning Disneyland?

I am a simple soul and one of my shortcomings is that I cannot see structure through a model that represents a series of tributaries; a core with many tendrils snaking from it. I, like so many fellow professionals, had become confused by the system we were being told to work to because it had become such a model. If we were going to develop a more creative curriculum, we would need to create a new, far simpler model. We also needed to define what a creative curriculum was. What we knew was that it couldn't develop as part of the existing system, like an 'add on' or afterthought.

The minute you mention the word 'creativity', particularly in relation to education, you are entering a minefield of misunderstanding – there are many misconceptions and interpretations. It is perhaps easier to explore what creativity is *not* in terms of educational development.

I know of schools that claim to be leaders in developing the creative curriculum. They ensure that their children 'do' more art, music, dancing, drama. They have a 'creativity day' every so often or a 'creativity week' every term. Some schools do 'creativity' every Friday as a treat if the class has worked hard.

It is true that we can find creativity and creative expression in the arts, but 'doing the arts' is not necessarily creative. It also dangerously assumes that creativity is a subject, a simple skill or competency that can be taught and is also the preserve of the arts.

A few years ago, I attended a UNESCO conference on Arts Education. It was an extraordinary experience. One of the speakers at the conference was a member of the Japanese delegation. He brilliantly exemplified one of the key problems with the teaching of the arts in our schools. He held up examples of portraits drawn by a class of elementary-age pupils. Many were skilfully rendered and colourful, but they were all essentially the same picture. The teacher had shown them how to do it and had shown them what she wanted, so the children worked faithfully towards a predestined outcome. This is clearly not creative. Neither is teaching children to sing a song in music; it may produce a lovely sound and skilled performers but it is not a creative process.

The big issue, however, is the misunderstanding that the very term 'creativity' in education sparks fears of the freedoms of the 1960s and 1970s and of some kind of non-academic arts fest.

The creative curriculum is a curriculum that is really no different from any other form of curriculum. It contains the same key learning, information, skills, competencies and the outline of knowledge and experiences. The creativity comes from the way it is introduced and developed with the children. In essence, it must be flexible, responsive to need and, most crucially of all, focused on developing children's natural sense of enquiry, hypothesis and investigation. It must be developmental but open-ended enough to allow children to find space and time to feed their imaginations and their thirst to find out new things in new ways, so that it feels constantly fresh and challenging. It must empower the children and ensure that they have a profound sense of ownership. There must be the security and opportunity for them to develop new thinking, new ideas and new directions of enquiry.

People talk of the challenge of 'developing' creativity as if it is some skill to be learned; the All Our Futures report identifies four key characteristics of creativity:

1. Thinking or behaving imaginatively
2. Imaginative activity is purposeful; it must be directed to achieving an objective
3. It must generate something original
4. The outcome must be of value to the objective

These are characteristics that we are born with, so the key aim of developing a curriculum that is creative is to ensure that at its heart is the notion that by helping our children to learn new skills and develop new competencies they will, given a richness of experiences and a climate of discovery, develop a desire for, and acquisition of, new knowledge that will feed their creative process ensuring that they constantly question, look for new pathways and solutions, think critically and have the confidence to generate fresh ideas.

At Grange we needed a model to make sense of the new process we were hoping to create. It had to conform to the statutory require-ments we were working with, but it also had to have a real sense of purpose. Rather than working with the existing model of National Curriculum as the main river and with strategies, both governmental and broader, being tributaries running off it in a multitude of directions, our model had to be simple and it had to be cyclical. It also had to be a model that was, by its nature, constantly able to evolve. To create a fixed model would immediately render it out of date, in the same way that any National Curriculum finds itself out of date as soon as it is published.

We arrived at a model that had, at its core, the development of our pupils as people and to that end it has four key elements:

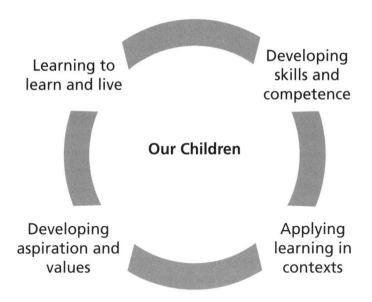

The Grange Primary School educational process model

Over the next few chapters I will look at the four elements and how they pull together to create a learning experience that meets many of the concerns raised through Section 1 of the book.

CHAPTER 14

Developing the whole child

Putting personal development at the heart of the process

Children are not empty vessels waiting to be filled to the brim with knowledge. They must not be judged by how much 'stuff' they can hold. After all fire wasn't discovered by an A-grade student!

Author

So for generations the focus of education has been the learning of new things, mainly concepts and information. We learnt our times tables by rote, we learned to do long division and fractions using textbooks, we learnt that there are 365 days in a year and that King Henry VIII of England had six wives, some of whom met a sticky end. All of this we learnt by teachers telling us.

However, we now know that what is deemed important information today may not be important tomorrow. What is certain is that the skills to take on and understand knowledge are permanent.

Maybe most crucially the top-down view of educational development, teacher's as providers of the facts, the wisdom, the knowledge, and pupils as the recipients, leads to a state where children become increasingly passive learners whose creative processes are slowly diminished as they start to see that learning is simply a right or a wrong, that the teacher will give them what they need. This leads to learners losing that magical sense of empowerment they are born with. The sense of empowerment is key as it provides the momentum for real learning, for a sense of worth and belonging and, most importantly, a confidence to engage and develop.

Over the three years I have been writing this book I, like billions of people around the world, have been transfixed by the rise of Barack Obama. On 4 November 2008 he swept to victory in the US presidential election and on 20 January 2009 took up office, to write a whole new chapter in world history. What has impressed me most is the way he has transfixed a new generation and helped people of all ages, faiths and backgrounds discover the power of politics and the impact of history. His now immortal mantra of change, which has been underpinned by a nation's new sense of empowerment, purpose and context, has been so much the secret to his success. He invested huge time, energy and money in connecting with the young and disenfranchised through the realms of new media in order to draw them in and generate, not just a sense of excitement and value, but a sense that they mattered and that change was not about him, or what he could do, but was how the United States as a nation, as a collection of individuals, could work together to create something new, to overcome the significant issues facing them and the rest of the world. Obama's trick has, in essence, been to give people back a sense that they are in charge of their own destiny and, by so doing, he has reinvigorated the most powerful country on earth. There is a profound lesson for us all here about how we need to connect to young people in order to have the same impact on them educationally.

We are led to believe that children can only learn if they are seated in front of a dynamic teacher. Indeed the film producer Lord Putnam, a huge advocate and champion of the teaching profession, some years ago suggested that out of work actors could help plug the shortfall in the teaching profession. I recall watching the news recently and seeing some 'teaching expert' suggest that all teachers should be given performance training similar to that of actors. This presupposes that the best way to learn new things is to have it imparted to you by a teacher. To be told is the pinnacle of learning. You cannot deny that an entertaining teacher is always better than a grey, monotone one. A good salesman will usually make a sale, but if the product is exciting enough and you want it anyway, you know you are going to purchase before you enter the shop.

If we rely on teachers to deliver our learning, how is it that most human learning occurs before the age of 3, before you are aware that schools, let alone teachers, even exist?

Teachers are a vital part of the learning process. Their professionalism, experience and passion are vital to any successful school, but our fixation that teachers are the deliverers of all learning is fundamentally flawed. I have so often seen a teacher inspire a child to learn and then seen that child go to another teacher who has a different style and that child shuts down, because of a personality clash. I have often seen highly successful children make fantastic progress when fronted by a teacher who is a teller of all, only to see them flounder horribly in higher education because the onus is on them to learn for themselves and they don't know how to do it. Teachers can unlock the gates but the pathways must have their own magic. Truly great teachers possess the ability to inspire interest and then create learning which allows children to explore, question and discover for themselves. Great teachers inspire and then empower.

Empowerment is key to learning

Our job as educators is to ensure that our children feel that they are responsible for their learning and that it is they who have the power to control their own lives.

At Grange we didn't want our children to behave because they were told to but because they wanted to. Similarly, we wanted our children to learn because they wanted to and we didn't want them to rely on the teacher to do that learning. If you go in to a through school, complete with an early years unit, you will see an interesting pattern emerging. In the nursery the children are afforded a great deal of independence; they will self-select activities and be carrying out investigations into pattern, shape, space, sound, colour, communication. They are not sitting in front of a teacher listening. They inherently know how to learn, they explore, question and develop. As you walk through a primary/elementary school, you see less evidence of this until, eventually, you see teachers standing in front of children talking. We are not developing independent learning strategies, we are almost suppressing them. For children to become skilled learners we must work with them to help them understand their natural instincts to learn and help them to develop those instincts and skills to be able to deploy them throughout life. Then they not only aid the learning process, but develop into the skills that show the initiative, innovative thinking, creative problem-solving and independence lacking in our emergent workforce.

Unfortunately, it is sometimes against our basic instincts to nurture learning correctly. We have all been guilty when our child is struggling to answer something of giving them the answer. When we hear our child read at home and they come across a word they don't know, we tell them the word almost by reflex. We should be encouraging our child to use clues to help them find the solution: sound it out. Does the picture help us? Read the rest of the sentence to see which word would help the sentence make sense.

It is vital, therefore, that at the heart of any school's curriculum must lie the development and understanding of how we learn and live. We don't have to build their houses for them, we can give them the tools we have helped them to use and they can build their own house, as creatively as they like.

Although this may seem like a gargantuan, and even abstract, task, it isn't, thanks to the research and development of learning to learn methodologies, led by a number of eminent educationalists including Howard Gardner, Alistair Smith and Guy Claxton. Helping children to understand how best they learn is not just the development of skills and competencies, it is also about the growing understanding of how personal wellbeing, environment and health can affect our readiness and ability to learn.

It is vital that our children learn about how their brains work and how their environment can impact on their own learning. There are many books written to help teachers and parents understand these vital platforms for learning and the principles are the same. So much of being a successful learner relies on our emotional state, our environment, knowing how our different brains function.

It is very interesting that the British government has begun to acknowledge this formally in the last few years, most powerfully in its

Every Child Matters agenda, which was published in 2005. Through its stress on multiagency working – health, social services, education – this ensured that the education establishment were committed to developing our children's welfare holistically in order to ensure that our children enjoy and succeed in their lives. There is a clear recognition that the learning journey is broader than a knowledge-driven curriculum. There is a clear recognition that schools must use their resources to develop facilities that address the challenge of helping our young learn to learn *and* live.

Nurture suites – cuddly nonsense or vital tool?

If we are lucky, as children, we grew up in loving home units surrounded by friends and family who encouraged and supported us and created conditions perfect for us to grow. As a result, we will have developed as confident and emotionally secure people. Sadly, this is not the case for all people and, increasingly, in a more and more fractured world the conditions are changing and are becoming more and more difficult for people to achieve. Emotional security is a vital factor in the success of a child's learning journey. The vast majority of children who struggle within the system do so because of an inability to understand and express their own feelings and a fundamental lack of self-worth.

It is important that we understand the workings of our brain. For example, one part our brain, known as the reptilian section, controls our fundamental emotional reflexes. So, if you encounter a situation that is unexpected, unfamiliar or surprising, you often feel the urge to run away. You sometimes freeze or you may become aggressive. It is inevitable that in any learning journey in which children are encouraged to explore and investigate beyond their known world, in conditions that can at times appear threatening, that these behaviours show themselves. If we can help children understand these emotions, then we can help them to recognize and, therefore, control them.

At Grange we developed a Nurture Suite, known as the Jigsaw Room. The facility was designed and run by two highly trained and skilled members of our staff. The facility was set out like a studio flat; it had a fully equipped kitchen area, a soft furnished lounge and an activity/living area. Children were invited to work through carefully designed processes in order to develop their own self-worth, their abilities to work in teams and to understand and to celebrate their own strengths and weaknesses. Children selected for the programme included a selective mute, children high on the autistic spectrum, aggressive children and emotionally insecure children who had suffered some kind of emotional trauma. The children spent a considerable time during the programme in the facility and the results were extraordinary. Those children made huge progress, impacting on their ability to develop as learners and as young members of the school community. One of these was the child who was a selective mute who would speak to no-one. Less than a year after beginning the programme, they took a key speaking part in the nativity play and performed amazingly.

The Nurture Suite is a clear example of the underpinning success of the approach. Without the commitment and focus of putting basic skills and knowledge first, formal education is wasted. The children in our facility who had not been able to go through the programme would still be identified as 'problem children' and poor learners.

The suite produced a fascinating and powerful by-product too. Unsurprisingly, we were aware that a number of our vulnerable children came from homes where their parents had poor school experiences and, as a result, were themselves somewhat school-phobic and, more importantly, in need of some support. Parents became curious about the suite, as it was easily accessible and looked nothing like a classroom. Some parents who were collecting their children from the facility at the end of the day would pop their heads around the door. The skill of the staff in encouraging and working with vulnerable children soon had the same effect on their parents, who started to use the facility with equal success which of course impacted on the children in very positive terms.

The key, however, was not the suite. It was the underpinning under-standing among the team that conditions for learning are the priority. In order to help our children thrive, they must know how they function best. For example, a child that cannot sit still is not necessarily disruptive; they may need physical stimulation to aid their concentration. The child who needs to see something before they understand it, rather than just have it explained to them, is a visual learner.

Let there be music

I work best when I have music playing in the background. When I was a headteacher, I had a CD system playing throughout the day in my office. I do the same in my office at home; it helps me to concentrate. I have colleagues who need to work in silence. I work well sitting next to a window and when the temperature is on the cool side; I know others who don't. This is the beauty of individuals. The important thing is that we know how we function best and alter our surroundings to help us achieve our most productive states. I have learnt this over time and have only really understood it since I began to explore brain-based learning for myself.

Imagine the power of the learner and the learning environment if our children were able to understand these conditions for themselves. Indeed, it is out of this new learning that we began to allow children drinks in their classrooms: if a brain becomes dehydrated, it cannot function as well.

Looking back on your schooling, were you the kind of child who would frequently be told off for twiddling your pencil? Do you now doodle on a scrap of paper when you are on the phone? These are not bad traits or 'ticks', they are positive reinforcements of your thinking process.

Learning is an intensely personal experience. We are all unique and, therefore, to each of us, every experience can mean different things, spark different emotions and different intellectual responses. The fact that we are all unique defines us as a species. For education to help us continue our evolution we must ensure that it helps us to develop that sense of who we are and how we fit within a wider community. For that reason LEARNING TO LEARN AND LIVE must form the foundation of our educational experience.

CHAPTER 15

Beyond subjects

Developing a thematic approach

Who invented Literacy?

Author

The world of subject-based teaching has put a huge constraint on the development of the education system for our children. As I have already discussed, it creates a fragmented and abstracted view of the world and it, therefore, makes the development of skills and competencies in our children disjointed and artificial.

Of course, there is a need to teach our children key skills that serve to aid their intellectual and social development. The basic skills and competencies related to communication and numeracy are at the core of all success for our young. If they lack these skills they will find it increasingly difficult to function in the world of today, let alone tomorrow. There is no argument that the development of literate and numerate children must lie at the heart of any learning journey. Thought and change are needed in defining the structure of that learning journey and maybe, more contentiously, how we teach these basic skills.

I have been fascinated by the Harry Potter phenomenon, as I believe that J. K. Rowling and her tales of teenage wizardry and heroism have led to a huge resurgence in reading, not just among our children, but among adults. Sadly, I believe that policy makers' attempts to improve the academic development of Literacy led to isolated strategies that were over-prescriptive and too complex. As a result, they have led to at least two generations of children being put off books and reading in conventional forms. As a child, I loved reading until I started my A-level English course, when I became fed up at being told to dissect books, to look for inner meaning and complexity, when I actually had read the books for entertainment, for enjoyment. I still refuse to believe that authors of the classics intellectualized their own books to the degree that academics have done. If you gave Shakespeare a copy of York Notes on one of his plays, would he say, 'Oh yes, that's exactly what I meant when I was writing *Romeo and Juliet.*'?

To many policy teams and academics, the development of literacy has meant the development of academic reading. Children as young as 5 are now dissecting books in the way we were taught, at the time of our exams, at 16 (O levels). When my children pick up books at home, they do so to find enjoyment, to escape to other worlds, to discover new things, not to study authorial intent. To some, this may be of interest, but to the fragile mind of a 10 year old, there is nothing less exciting or rewarding. We live in a world dominated by new media. Theatre directors and successful writers have realized this and, as a result, have responded by developing far more 'cinematic' approaches to their work in order to attract the mass market. One of the most powerful examples for me is the work of the crime novelist James Patterson, whose writing is developed in short, film-style paragraphs, which creates pace and purpose for a reader, similar to the familiar visual media that dominate our world.

So why is Harry Potter so successful? I am sure that there will be studies made in detail, but for me, two factors stand out: first, that the books are written about children today, even though they are set in a world of magic and largely in a parallel world. The children are modern kids, often fighting against a mysterious world that they are having to adapt into and that strange world is largely set in the grounds of their school, Hogwarts. Many children will be able to identify with that today. They go to school, they are taught subjects which often use strange vocabulary and about things that are a step divorced from their own reality and experience. The second factor is that J. K. Rowling's books have never featured in the lists of books to be taught in the Literacy hour. It is interesting that for some time after the publication of the Literacy Framework in the UK, fewer children were reading Roald Dahl; his work was on the list of suggested texts in the Literacy hour.

Our current curricular structure does not develop our interests in our cultures and heritage. It does not develop our children as lifelong learners. For the vast majority, it has the opposite effect. It turns us off. We cannot allow this to continue. The reasons the problem seems to be accelerating among our children is because they have a greater breadth of choice as to how to spend their time and, unless we fire their imaginations and spark their interest, they will opt out at the earliest opportunity.

Sometime ago I met a school's parent governor who was very wound up, at a conference. It transpired that before leaving for the event he had had a blazing row with his son over GCSE options for the following year. His son, a gifted musician and First Violin in the regional youth orchestra, had told his father that he was not taking up GCSE Music. Naturally, his father was amazed and frustrated; a row followed, during which the boy turned to his father and justified his decision by saying, 'Dad, I love music, it is my passion, my life. If I take that GCSE course it will destroy my love for it!'

The biggest challenge, therefore, is not just to provide learning opportunities that inform but, through the acquisition of knowledge and experiences, through the development of skills, explicitly add to the quality of our children's lives, not just as a future goal but for now.

What I did at school today – a day in the life of a child in school

When the bell went, I lined up on the playground with my class. I stood next to Jake. We were just about to put our collector cards away when they were confiscated. We are not allowed them at school because our headteacher says we don't know how to share and swaps always end in arguments.

When we got into class, Miss told us to sit down and do the sum on the board while she did the register. I hate division and the sum was hard, because it was share by 8 and I've only learnt up to the 5 times table. Still, I copied Sammy's because she is in Lions group and they are on their 9s.

When Miss called my name, I said, 'Here' and gave her the envelope with my dinner money in.

We had assembly where we sang a song, did a prayer and listened to a story about Jesus. My bum was sore because we were sitting on the floor as usual. Tommy got told off for fidgeting with his new shoes; he's got Velcro rather than laces. My trousers itched.

In Literacy we did biographies again, like yesterday and the day before. We started by reading a page together about Beckham. The book was dead old, in the picture of him he still had a Mohican hair cut. After reading, we went back to our desks and had to underline all the doing words. I got told off because I used a green pencil and I was supposed to use red.

At break we ran out on to the playground. We tried to get out first so that we could get the football area, but the Year 6s got there first, so we had to watch. I ended up play-fighting with Todd, but I hurt him in the eye by accident and had to spend the rest of playtime standing against the wall.

In Numeracy we started with our warm-up. I enjoy that because I get to scribble on a little board with a pen. My bum still hurts though, because we are sitting on the floor again. Then we did the counting stick again and then we did some sums. Miss worked with Tigers because they are the slow group; they can't even do their 3 times tables yet!

Lunch was okay, we get pizza on Wednesdays. It was cold on the playground and Year 6 had got the football again. We ran around a bit. When the bell went I was glad to get in to the warm. Miss did the register and we did silent reading. I'm still reading the red books which are boring, Miss says that I can move on to blue books if I finish all the books on red shelf. I don't like reading, it's boring, and I prefer my PSP.

Afternoon was alright. First we did some history about the Victorians. We watched a programme on the TV and had to make notes about it in our rough books. I drew a picture of a Power Ranger, Miss didn't find out.

Last lesson was Technology; we did buggies. We did them in Year 2 as well, but these ones were for pulling coal out of the mines.

Tomorrow will be the same except in the afternoon we are doing databases in ICT. I'd rather add some content to my Facebook, and PE in the afternoon; damn, I've lost my kit!

So much of our children's school days are like ours, but we have done nothing to change them. Yes, there have been new government strategies but they are all devised to work within the existing structure. The vast majority are cosmetic and been designed and delivered by people who are long distanced from children, and the changes have been designed to develop the measures aimed at the status quo.

Our curricula and timetables must be filled with flexibility, we must surprise and entertain. We must create experiences that build platforms for our children that are based on skills and the opportunity to develop those skills, to apply them in interesting ways that relate to their lives now and in the future.

40 or 50 years ago, there was a belief that we must limit children's experiences and learning at an early age, as to give them too much to think about was dangerous for them. Of course we know that this is nonsense. If we don't stimulate and challenge our children's brains will not develop to their potential. Take the child growing up in a multilingual household; they will absorb every language spoken in that

home, no matter how many, and will become proficient in them all. The child growing up in a monolingual home will learn one language only. Trying to teach them other languages in later life becomes far more difficult because some of their language acquisition ability has deteriorated.

We patronize our children and their abilities to absorb, process and use learning.

At Grange we needed to design a new approach to the curriculum and a learning journey that focused on the development of skills in contexts that allowed for flexibility of focus, real application and, most importantly, an end to abstract, isolated subject development. We wanted to create a curriculum that the children felt ownership of, that allowed them to apply newly acquired skills in ways that meant something to them now and in the future.

To do this we wanted to use the existing structure of curriculum applied in our early years department (pre-5 year olds) and develop it through the entire school in a way that held the key skills and competencies of Literacy and Numeracy at the heart, yet dispensed with the fragmented nature of the National Curriculum approach. We needed to find a way to build on the development of our underpinning learning to learn and live foundation.

We began by looking at the curriculum flexibly and as a resource to develop the learning and life skills. To that end we set about researching materials already in existence that would help us develop our framework. We found two that were of notable use to us. The first was The Opening Minds New Curriculum material first published in 1999 by the Royal Society for the Arts:

Opening minds key competencies
Developing a competence-led curriculum
In Opening Minds five categories of competences are proposed. Each category contains a number of individual competences, which are expressed in terms of what a school student could achieve, having progressed through the curriculum:

Competences for learning
Students would:
- Understand how to learn, taking account of their preferred learning styles, and understand the need to, and how to, manage their own learning throughout life.

- Have learned, systematically, to think.
- Have explored and reached an understanding of their own creative talents, and how best to make use of them.
- Have learned to enjoy and love learning for its own sake and as part of understanding themselves.
- Have achieved high standards in literacy, numeracy, and spatial understanding.
- Have achieved high standards of competence in handling information and communications technology and understand the underlying processes.

Competences for citizenship
Students would:

- Have developed an understanding of ethics and values, how personal behaviour should be informed by these, and how to contribute to society.
- Understand how society, government and business work, and the importance of active citizenship.
- Understand cultural and community diversity, in both national and global contexts, and why these should be respected and valued.
- Understand the social implications of technology.
- Have developed an understanding of how to manage aspects of their own lives, and the techniques they might use to do so – including managing their financial affairs.

Competences for relating to people
Students would:

- Understand how to relate to other people in varying contexts in which they might find themselves, including those where they manage, or are managed by others; and how to get things done.
- Understand how to operate in teams, and their own capacities for filling different team roles.
- Understand how to develop other people, whether as peer or teacher.
- Have developed a range of techniques for communicating by different means, and understand how and when to use them.
- Have developed competence in managing personal and emotional relationships.

- Understand, and be able to use, varying means of managing stress and conflict.

Competences for managing situations
Students would:
- Understand the importance of managing their own time, and have developed preferred techniques for doing so.
- Understand what is meant by managing change, and have developed a range of techniques for use in varying situations.
- Understand the importance both of celebrating success and managing disappointment, and ways of handling these.
- Understand what is meant by being entrepreneurial and initiative-taking, and how to develop capacities for these.
- Understand how to manage risk and uncertainty, the wide range of contexts in which these will be encountered, and techniques for managing them

Competences for managing information
Students would:
- Have developed a range of techniques for accessing, evaluating and differentiating information and have learned how to analyse, synthesize and apply it.
- Understand the importance of reflecting and applying critical judgement, and have learned how to do so.

While still quite abstract, it gave us a clear insight in to how to develop a skills-focused curriculum. We still had to meet the statutory requirements of the National Curriculum which, surprisingly, are considerably fewer than most schools or parents imagine. In order to do that, we stumbled across an invaluable piece of work developed by Somerset local authority called 'Curriculum Planning for Schools', which set out the National Curriculum in a highly defined skills format, but still subject-based.

The most challenging step for us was to reinvent the delivery mechanisms, the timetable and, most importantly, the reorganization of a curriculum that was not to be punctuated by subject, but by skills and competencies.

We designed a curriculum that had at its core four strands:

1. Communication
2. Enterprise
3. Culture
4. Wellbeing

Communication had the development of Literacy at its heart, but drew on wider communication skills that included the use of ICT, dance, drama, music etc.

Enterprise had the development of Numeracy at its core and applied those skills in wider contexts, to include problem-solving and innovation.

Culture had Science at its heart, as the lifeblood for understanding our world and our place within it, but expanded to focus on the traditional cultural aspects of our heritage, rooted in History and Geography.

Wellbeing was the final, vital component in our system. We wanted to raise the profile and importance of physical and mental health in our system in order to fully prepare our children for the future. It had physical education at its heart, but existed to tie in many aspects from the citizenship and social education areas, as well as the centre of our commitment to emotional development. As a result, it was split into the three areas of physical, social and spiritual wellbeing.

Lit and Num 20s replaced the discrete Literacy and Numeracy hours running in most schools; most of our Literacy and Numeracy would be covered through contextual application in the Communication and Enterprise sections of the day, but there was a definite need to teach the key skills and concepts independently. Notionally the sessions were 20 minutes in length and were high-intensity, teacher-driven sessions. They were flexible though, allowing teachers to extend the length of the sessions should they feel that the children needed more input and reinforcement.

We also needed to explore the methodology for the approach, in order to draw the best out of the opportunities created by the four strands.

We wanted to wrap the approach in really flexible and realistic experiences that would provide a quality of experience that would support the development of all. We wanted to develop weeks that would be a little unpredictable and, to an extent, governed by the route the journey was developing. It is important to stress at this stage, however, that the entire process is underpinned by the clear development of learning and life skills, competencies and curricular concepts that our children need to develop successfully. The process was also planned to respond to the assessed needs of each and every child.

Vital to the next stage of our development was that our curriculum would not serve as just another exercise in academic development, but would genuinely seek to find and develop each child's unique skills and interests, equipping them with real insights into their own future needs and aspirations.

To help with the explanation of the model I have used a timetable illustration (*see page 122*).

The approach was flexible and allowed for staff and pupils to define themes that fuelled the approach. Each school year the school community decided on themes for each term that would work as overarching, whole-school themes. They were deliberately large and abstract and might include Tomorrow's World or Travel. Each class teacher then worked with his or her class to decide how they wanted to explore the whole-school theme. The teacher would then work through a planning framework to marry the learning and living skills and competencies with the National Curriculum entitlement, the Literacy and Numeracy strategies and the agreed content. The class would then work through the topic using the four strands to provide structure.

The travel scenario

Using travel as the theme a class might decide to set up and run a travel agency for the duration of the topic. In the Communication strand they might investigate travel brochures, both paper and electronic versions. They would research and develop their own and explore marketing and advertising strategies to promote their new agency.

In the Enterprise strand they would explore the cost of holidays and the different elements of the costings, from travel arrangements to accommodation options, as well as pricing structures. They would also explore measures and distance within a geographical context.

Using the Cultural strand, the teachers and children would explore how the vehicles of travel work: how planes fly, boats float and trains function. They would explore the historical and geographical contexts of the places they were looking to sell as holidays.

New Curriculum Building Blocks	SESSION 1		SESSION 2		SESSION 3		SESSION 4	
MONDAY	Weekly Briefing		Lit 20	Communication Focus	Num 20	Enterprise Focus	Wellbeing	School Council Assembly @ 2:40pm
TUESDAY	Lit 20	Communication Focus	Num 20	Enterprise Focus	ICT Skills		Culture Focus	
WEDNESDAY	Num 20	Enterprise Focus	Lit 20	Communication Focus	Culture Focus		Learn Share	Midweek review
THURSDAY	Lit 20	Communication Focus	Num 20	Enterprise Focus	Culture Focus		Skills Enhancement Session (L2L)	
FRIDAY	Grange University Workshops		Grange University Workshops		Wellbeing		Weekly Debrief and Our World this Week	

New curriculum building blocks

The Wellbeing strand would provide a context for exploring the environmental impact of travel and holidays and alternative health-based breaks, as well as providing opportunities to try out sports and games from the different countries featured. They would also explore the religious heritage of some of their chosen holiday destinations.

Surrounding the approach, the timetable had various other strands which supported the development of the children, their skills and their contexts.

Learn share

This was developed from the need to help our children communicate and empathize with others. In most schools children tend to work and play with the children of their own age, in their own class. We wanted to ensure that our children began to see themselves as a whole-school community and to be able to develop skills that allowed them to empathize and interact with other children outside their usual grouping. Learn Share evolved out of a weekly session where children throughout the school were paired with a child from another class and year group and would work with them to share reading. The system proved so successful that we expanded it to allow children to share all aspects of their learning and, indeed, their interests. Because the school was now running overarching themes, this became salient to every child. At a set time each week each twinned class would pair up so that the partnered children would have time together. The next stage of development would be to have 'themed' weeks where the partners would be encouraged to share hobbies, collections or music for example. Crucially, the children spent time with others from different backgrounds and levels of experience which would have a massive social impact on them, their peers and, indeed, the whole school community.

Our world this week

During the events of the Boxing Day Tsunami in 2004 we realized that our children had been hugely affected, thanks in part to the enormous multi-media coverage. Sadly, we realized that many of them had a limited understanding of, or way to contextualize, the news and stories in front of them. The same had been true at the time of 9/11 and was true of the 7/7 bombings a year later. We felt that, due to the enclosed nature of schools, children were not relating their lives to the lives of the global population in real terms and so we introduced a 'current affairs' session at the end of every week in every class. Run like a circle time, the session's content was defined by the children themselves. Each week the children would bring in news items that had caught their interest in the past week, from newspapers, the internet or television. They discussed the items and peoples' feelings towards them. The teacher would help to provide a context. At the end of the discussions the items were placed in a class archive that built up over the year to provide a record of the world's events during the children's time in any class. The archives were then centralized and used as a resource.

ICT skills

One of the most noticeable changes in children since the mid 1990s has been their natural understanding of new technologies. Whereas we used to have to teach children what a computer was, how to turn it on and how to use a mouse, today 3-year-olds in our nurseries know exactly how to control the technology. Therefore, the need for discrete lessons in ICT is diminishing. Indeed, I would argue that to persist with timetabled ICT sessions will become counter-productive. Technology is a tool, not a subject. Use of technology is central to our philosophy of developing a system equipped for the future and, to that end, we need all of our children to have access, on demand, to the tools that form part of the fabric of their everyday lives. I now know of many schools who are developing fantastic approaches to on-demand technology access. We worked hard to provide every child with handheld computer equipment that would provide wireless access to the internet and the network, wherever they were in the school. Because handheld technologies develop so fast we did retain some discrete time in the timetable to ensure that, should they need it, time was made available for learning about the new technologies at our pupils' disposal. Children should not be getting hand-me-down technology, but should have access to cutting-edge technologies that they can use, develop and carry with them into the adult world. Computer suites have increasingly limited use. Schools should now be investing in cutting-edge, handheld technologies, where possible using technology already at children's disposal. PSPs have wireless internet capability. If the school has a wireless network pupils can use their own devices to work with. The dreaded mobile phone can be used similarly, as well as using their camera and video functionality.

We began to explore the use of text-message challenges and support for our children directly to their phones.

The final key element of the timetable was the development of the Grange University, which I will expand on later in the book.

The playground vacuum

Another major part of the school experience we wanted to work on was the experience for our children during 'free time'. So many of us remember our own playtime experiences with mixed emotions. Yes, they were times to escape work and the teachers. Yes, they were times for playing football, swapping collectables and talking, but they were often cold, empty times, especially for the children who didn't like football or for the kids who wanted a place to talk and interact in comfort. Lunchtimes were often the worst times; after eating, you could be left with an hour-long vacuum of space, time and frostbite. Grange was just like this and, unsurprisingly, most of the fights and bad behaviour occurred at this time. Why is it acceptable to force kids into conditions and environments that we, as adults, would not wish to endure?

If we were going to develop real independence and responsibility in our children, we needed to give them the opportunity to learn and to experience the benefits of that independence and the responsibility that came with it.

We decided to open up all of our facilities to the children at lunchtimes: the library, the ICT suite, the adventure playground and various options linked to the Grangeton Project, which I will expand upon in the next chapter. This meant that our children could elect to stay and play on the playground, or elect to do something else. They had to choose a different option every day so that they were not able to stagnate.

The impact was extraordinary. The children responded fantastically to the freedom of choice and growth of breaktime options, which led to a vast reduction in poor behaviour and saw a tangible improvement in one of our key learning and life objectives, independence.

If a school is to really develop a skills- and competency-driven curriculum, it cannot impose it on its existing structures. It must reinvent its entire approach. It means that there must be a commitment to developing every aspect of school life with equal vigour. There must be a real awareness that some of the most important learning for children, particularly in their holistic development, occurs outside the structured teaching sessions and that real investment needs to be made in those times.

It is crucial that schools set realistic expectations of their staff and children and relax in the knowledge that tangible change takes time. Children will not become more independent or responsible just because a new policy has been agreed and implemented and there will be setbacks and disappointments. As a school, the community must stick with development programmes and realize that attitudinal change takes time. After all, we have worked in a fixed way, with fixed perceptions for a very long time and that kind of ingrained conditioning does not alter overnight. The key is to have the courage of your convictions, stick with the learning and life skills focus and there will be dramatic change in time. Don't be tempted to change tack because results aren't apparent in the short term.

CHAPTER 16

The Grangeton Project

Creating three-dimensional learning

Learning MUST matter to the learner. For it to matter it must have relevance and context. I learned to walk so that I could get to the cookie jar in the kitchen. I learned to drive a car so that I could go places my parents didn't know about . . . maybe it's selfish but what *is* in it for me?

Author

The Grangeton Shop

My son is at the peak of the 'But why?' phase in his development. I have never felt under so much pressure as a parent: why is the sun hot? Because it's a ball of fire and gas. But why is it fire and gas? Because . . . but why?

A day or so after starting school, my son and I had one of those philosophical discussions you can only have with a 5 year old:

'Daddy, I like school.'
'Great. It's fun isn't it?'
'Yeah, but why do I have to go every day?'
'Because it will help you learn stuff.'
'Why do I need to learn stuff?'
'Because it's important and it's fun.'
'Playing at home is fun. Why is it important?'
'Because it will help you grow up to be clever.'
'But Mummy says that I am already clever. She always says that I'm her clever little boy.'
'You are, darling, and if you work hard at school you will be able to get a good job when you are older.'
'Will they teach me to be Andy Murray then, because that's what I'm going to be when I grow up?'

And so the conversation goes on. Young children learn through imitation, play and role play and the amazing thing is they grow to do it naturally; it is how they acquire language. It is actually how they begin to make sense of the world around them. We must build on that unique learning facet at school and do more to make learning matter to our children. For me, the power of a learning journey comes when a young person has a growing awareness of who they are and what they can do. The magic comes when our children grow to see what they are capable of and can see that the skills they have and the ones they are developing can make a positive difference to their world. When a child learns to walk the pleasure on their faces and on your face as they take those first steps, is one of life's truly magic moments. The first time they employ sound to make a recognized word is a place locked in our hearts. It brings pleasure, a recognition that something new has just been mastered and it is about to make my world better. Now I can walk, I can go where I want; now that I can speak, I can be understood. So when I learn that the capital of England is London, I can . . . ?

We must wrap learning in contexts that allow children to celebrate newly acquired skills and immediately demonstrate the benefits to them and to their future.

We must also ensure that the learning is seen as relevant; it builds on their experiences and makes sense. It must be pleasurable, memorable and important. It is no good telling children and hoping that by doing so enough, or with enough force, they will 'get it'. As a species we are self-centred. There must always be a 'What's in it for me?' Skilled educators realize that and the most successful teachers empathize with their children, understand their world and use it to create magical learning journeys. The teachers we remember as children made us 'feel our learning', helped us to develop emotional attachment to the journey.

At Grange we wanted to do two things: we wanted to engage our kids in the journey and make it matter. We also wanted to expand their horizons and design opportunities to see how newly developed skills could be used in the world around them, so that they could celebrate their achievements and stimulate them to further their development. A perfect learning circle; you try to stand, fall over, bump your bottom and your knees, but you keep on trying because you know it will be worth it in the end.

We also wanted to make learning immediate and real, building on their world, their experiences and their interests.

Sensory learning

We have all been somewhere and recognized a smell that has evoked a past memory; it can transport us back to another time, another place. For me, it is certain types of cleaning fluids, don't ask me why! For some, it is the smell of freshly baked bread, coffee, boiled cabbage. The incredible thing is not only does it lead to a memory, but it also wells up the emotional memory of the event. The same thing can happen with sounds, particularly music. Our senses have huge power and are underused as learning tools in schools.

In 2004 a team led by Jay Gottfried of University College London's Department of Imaging Neuroscience produced a comprehensive study of memory retrieval. The researchers claimed that memories relating to an event are scattered across the brain's sensory centres but marshalled by a region called the hippocampus. If one of the senses is stimulated to evoke a memory, other memories featuring other senses are also triggered.

This explains why a familiar song or the smell of a former lover's perfume have the power to conjure up a detailed picture of past times. Gottfried says:

> That's the beauty of our memory system; imagine a nice day on the beach. The smell of sun lotion, the friends you were with, the beer you were drinking; any of these could trigger memories of the whole thing.

(J. A. Gottfried, Neuron, 42, pages 687–695)

Using the senses to help create memory tags and to create three-dimensional learning experiences were methods that I had explored for most of my career and they were approaches that the staff at Grange took on and developed by:

* Creating 'smelloramic' displays, as opposed to visual ones. Creating displays, particularly in corridors, that evoke the sense of a topic through smell and sound rather than relying purely on image – the seaside, for example. or even Tudor England!
* Using music to exemplify to children how the length of a sentence in a piece of writing can affect the mood of the reader, by using film music to demonstrate how a viewer can be affected by a soundtrack; the way the 'dada, dada, dada' in *Jaws* becoming quicker and quicker builds tension, and explaining how by using short phrases and sentences you can create the same effect in writing.
* Utilizing taste to help children understand and remember fractions. Giving them all a few chocolate buttons and explaining wholes, halves and quarters by letting them place one button in their mouth and asking them how it feels, then letting them do the same thing with two and explaining to them that the difference in 'chocolatiness' is the difference between a quarter and a half and then, as a finale, allowing them to place four in their mouth and explaining that that, the ultimate taste sensation, was the difference between a half and a whole.

The Grangeton Project

When I took over the headship at Grange I wanted desperately to allow our children to apply their learning in real contexts, through what is now called 'applied learning'. The challenge was to capture those early childhood traits of enquiry, exploration, hypothesis and discovery. To do so by creating learning that was 'real', purposeful and immediate. It was also vitally important to find a way that would very quickly empower the children and, indeed, the whole school community, to develop a sense of ownership, of control, and to build a powerful momentum that came from a real sense of purpose.

In so many ways empowerment is the key to a great school. Maybe even more than that it is, perhaps, the key to a person having a successful and fulfilling life. Learning can so often feel beyond our control as children and as teachers and it is then that the magic dies;

when the frustration and even anger fester. Most sadly of all it is a lack of empowerment which can be the root cause of risk aversion. Most people, when they cross a road, feel relatively safe. In control, on a straight road, with good visibility, they control most of the parameters, anxiety levels are low. Driving a car, again most people feel relatively in control and, therefore, the anxiety is not too high. You feel a little more anxious than when crossing a road perhaps. Because you do not control other drivers, your empowerment is a little less. As passengers on an aeroplane, despite statistical logic, we are often at our most anxious because, not only can we not see where we are going, we have no control over our fate.

Grange was an anxious school where staff and pupils felt that they were not really in control. In fact, the lack of empowerment was at the heart of the school's struggle. It was therefore an imperative that our first major strategy responded to that.

It is often the way a new idea or strategy is implemented, rather than the quality of the idea or strategy itself, that can spell success or failure and this is never more acute than in a struggling organization like an underperforming school. The mistake that I think many organizations and schools make when under pressure to transform is to create a strategy lock, stock and barrel; to try and find the answers to all the potential questions and concerns by developing rigid systems before implementing change. Then leadership presents the system to the team and expects it to be implemented. Leadership does this, not out of power or control, but because they want to minimize anxiety and therefore resistance. In the short term in an environment where empowerment has not been a significant part of the culture, this strategy can have some success but will often lead to initiative overload and a dependency culture which becomes far too superficial for real transformation to take place.

We so often put pressure on ourselves to get results quickly, to see radical change overnight, that we become preoccupied with the outcome, rather than letting an idea develop as people are able to grasp the concept and then start to feed in to expand it. The most powerful form of empowerment in a school is the process of co-creation and that is what the Grangeton Project was. It was based on an idea; we wanted to create an opportunity for our children to utilize their learning in a real 'adult world' environment to help them understand the world around them, the opportunities available to them and the growing responsibility they would have as emerging citizens. As the ideas, concepts and projects developed it became clear to us that we were, in many ways, developing a micro-community that reflected the world beyond the gates and we wanted to exploit that view further by turning the school into a fully functioning town, managed and run by the children themselves, for the children.

And so Grangeton was born.

The town and experiences had to be authentic, they had to have real purpose and value, so we called on experts from our wider community to help us devise the concepts and design the training experiences. All the children at Grange were exposed to each of the elements of the town and encouraged to work within it.

The town included:

* A political system or council made up of elected representatives from throughout the school and chaired by a separately elected mayor, who also represented the pupils on the school's governing body. The mayor was elected by the pupil body, following an authentic and hard fought annual election campaign. The council and mayor received part of their training from their local Member of Parliament, which included a visit to the Palace of Westminster.
* An environmental team, who managed the physical environment, the ecology drive and the growing of fruit, vegetables and other plants for sale and use in the school's kitchen.
* A pupil buddy system trained pupils in conflict resolution, playground management, basic counselling and first aid. The trained pupils then worked to ensure safety and order at playtimes. They were trained in part by the local police and health services.

The town contained a number of enterprises that served the needs of the community and included:

* A franchise of healthy-eating shops managed and run by the children. The pupils were trained by a local supermarket chain.
* A café which served freshly prepared snacks at lunchtimes and was staffed and run by the pupils who were trained by local businesses in food preparation, hygiene and customer service. The café was a French-themed eatery where the menu was in French, the food was French inspired and the language spoken by the staff was French. This ensured not just a context for the café, but for the learning of modern foreign languages.

* A museum which charted the history of the school in the wider community and was open to the public as well as providing a powerful local history resource. The children were trained by the local museum staff and managed their museum within real guidelines.
* A craft centre/gift shop, next to the museum, which stocked and sold all manner of craft items, souvenirs and goods designed and manufactured by the children, including artwork which was displayed for sale in the adjoining gallery.
* Its own media centre which produced a newspaper, daily radio programme and various films and DVDs.

The town grew, as any real town does, with more and more children becoming involved. We had children as young as 7 years old running their own radio programmes and children in the Nursery shooting their own films.

A Grangeton movie project

The success of the town was extraordinary. It gave the children ownership of their school and it added a tangible sense of purpose to their learning and developed a sense of pride and responsibility that lead to their incredibly mature and independent attitudes. It was been crucial to the school's success.

What was important was not to limit the town's development or growth, based on our own naivety or fear of what we didn't know or couldn't do ourselves but to look beyond the gates for the expertise and skills needed to help make the experience occur and to give it authenticity. It is so easy to limit our children's learning to the depths of our own experiences or knowledge. We needed to be bigger and braver than that and that is where the entrepreneurial art of networking came in; applying the old adage of 'It's not what you know but who you know'.

We spent time and effort attracting people from the community to help us and were amazed at the positive response. The worst knockback we received was, 'Sorry, we can't help but I do know someone who may be interested.' As a result, within weeks we were linked to banks, broadcasters and businesses who were able to help us build our beautiful new town, and for free!

Initially we set the town up to be run and managed by our final year students; most of their time was taken up at breaktimes, lunchtimes, before and after school. Very quickly the pupils started to negotiate with their teachers to use certain lesson time too. This was done with the understanding from both staff and children that sometimes that would be alright and at other times it wouldn't. In order to create sustainability and in order to eventually hand over all core responsibility for the town to the pupils, we needed to develop potential from pupils throughout the school, so for three years every Friday afternoon we cleared our timetable from Nursery up to Year 6 and set up Grangeton afternoons. Each year group would spend half a term studying each enterprise, how they worked in the 'real world' and how they worked at Grange. They also spent time learning about the skills, competencies and knowledge they would need to work in any of the town's facilities. We bought in our external partners and used the 'expert' older children to help provide the experiences and learning. It wasn't long before the children had developed their interests and experiences of the town so that children from all year groups were confident enough to apply for jobs and train each other as part of the overriding culture of the school.

It was a matter of months before Grangeton had become the core of the school's practice, permeating both extracurricular and curricular practice. In the summer of 2008, nearly a year after I left, the school had its Ofsted inspection and was identified as outstanding in all areas. The report cited the Grangeton Project as a crucial factor in the school's success.

At Grange we took the learning model natural to young children, of play, mimicry and role play, and developed it through the system, so that it became more and more real. We have all put on 'shows' for our mums and dads, recorded 'radio shows' for them to listen to on our tape players and it is these things that we remember. Learning does not need to be painful, a sacrifice. All schools have the capacity and the ability to remodel their systems accordingly. The approach was not a trade off: fun or standards. One leads to the other. What I know is that the children who experienced Grangeton developed the confidence and skills to succeed. It was not only the children who developed an extraordinary sense of empowerment, but the staff too. It was a huge source of pride to us all, because we developed it together and, as a result, it was sustainable. It was immune to the curse of the implemented initiative destined to end up on the scrapheap of the 'been there done that' pile, left in an old forgotten storeroom under the stairs. The key, though, was taking little steps, of not knowing what the final outcome would be but knowing that, if the principles were right and that the journey was controlled by the team, we would get to somewhere very exciting . . . and we did.

CHAPTER 17

A curriculum of all the talents

Nurturing every individual and finding what makes them tick

Our schools must help our children to broaden their minds, feed their imaginations, develop their aspirations. Experiences are everything; without experiences we would live in very dark places.

Author

As children grow and become more independent, learning becomes more and more optional in their own minds. As soon as we take the scaffold of legal requirement away from the educational journey how many children continue their push, driven by desire to work towards their own future? How many opt out at the earliest opportunity to seek a different path? For me, education should not be a ship you leave to start a new journey; a rowing boat becomes a pleasure boat, becomes a ferry, becomes a cruise ship, becomes a tanker. The problem with boats is that if you fall off, you can drown. It should be a seamless progression. Learning should not be the preserve of education; education should be about developing the skills for life, one of which is the ability to learn. Learning should be a lifelong journey, punctuated by experiences, people and roles. Education should be about exploring and developing your interests and potential, to help you find your place in society, to help you find the route to maximize your own life.

I truly believe that formal education fails the majority of us, as it fails to find and develop our unique interests and aptitudes. To an extent schools are judgemental places that sift and sort children and help fire the desire of society to pigeon-hole and label. There is a hierarchy of outcomes that schools sell to prospective parents, as demonstrators of their success: Oxbridge pupils, former pupils who have become lawyers, judges, accountants and doctors, numbers of children who have attended university.

I was once told by a particularly supercilious and arrogant teacher that I would end up as nothing more than a 'bin man'. Why? I had just dropped History A level to spend more time on my Art and English. By dropping History, as far as he was concerned, I had underlined my intellectual inadequacy and was not deserving of a place in higher education. The insult was that I deserved nothing better than a job helping keep Britain tidy. I can think of worse.

We support young people's aspirations, but give them a sliding scale of importance. University is seen as the pinnacle of the system and those leaving to start jobs at 16 years old are seen as the failures.

The issues are not the making of secondary schools, but of the primary/elementary system and it is our responsibility to provide a wealth of opportunities to ensure that children can find their strengths, interests and vocations.

The government in the UK is obsessed with a 'gifted and talented' register, which is, for the most part, defined by children's academic progress. How could it be anything else? It is what schools do. I believe that every child has a gift, a talent; it is just that most go undiscovered. Tragically, if they are ever found, it is often too late.

People must have their talents and gifts nurtured from an early age. To do this, schools must create expansive opportunities to help our young people identify their talents, no matter what they may be.

Is it any wonder that in sport, as a nation, we lag behind so many countries, many much smaller than ourselves? Our system is not set up to provide opportunities to realize talent and to nurture it. It is just not a priority in our academic system.

In his book, *The Element*, Sir Ken Robinson interviewed many people identified as the most successful in their fields and disciplines, many of whom have become role models, some icons, for generations. The book explores human capacity and, in particular, the identification and nurturing of talent. Many of these people, upon reflection, say that formal education had little to do with helping them become the people they are today. Some talk about the negative impact of schooling on their development.

I have worked with some remarkable children who are challenged by standard academic education and are often labelled as 'special needs', but they exhibit extraordinary skills when it comes to designing and making things. Imagine their futures if they were given the opportunities to thrive.

I was at school with a boy who was obsessed by records and dance music; it is what he did in his spare time. The school passed him off as disruptive and of poor ability. He went on to become one of the world's first, and most famous, club DJs, earning ridiculous amounts of money in the process. If it wasn't for his own extraordinary resilience and passion, he would never have become the success he did. Imagine how many equally talented youngsters there are out there who have dropped out and have been missed.

At Grange we were determined to supplement Grangeton with a more expansive set of experiences and opportunities, to find the untapped potential in our children. To my mind it was vital for their development.

It is a fact that many children accelerate down the spiral of educational decline due to a growing lack of confidence and a rapidly declining sense of self-worth. They feel that they are failing the system and are therefore worthless. The key is to find the connection, the spark that fires that child. The child themselves may not know what it is but, if and when you find it, and the child has the opportunity to demonstrate their skill, potential and ability in their 'thing', their confidence can rapidly build and, with it, their engagement and success in mainstream schooling. The two go hand in hand.

It was important for us to break down the mystique of higher education as a preserve of the clever, the academically gifted and so we set out to combine the two.

Our response was the development of Grange University, which ran every Friday morning. The model was developed out of a story I had heard about the film animation organization Pixar, which actively encourages their staff to pursue personal development opportunities by giving them time during the working week to attend courses and training in order to develop that personal interest. It was a strategy designed to maximize the potential of their staff and therefore aid the productivity and success of their business.

Our university ran for two hours every week and offered the children throughout the school up to 40 different workshop options. They signed up to two each term and completed 12 options in every school year. Each option ran for 6 weeks, at the end of which each child received a level of accreditation depending on the level of skill and aptitude they demonstrated in each option. They collected their accreditations through their school career and they formed a holistic, career-entry profile which they could use at their secondary school and beyond to detail their skills and interests. At the end of their time at Grange, aged 11, they graduated from the university.

In order to accommodate such a large number of workshop options and to guarantee diversity, we worked with our community and our parents to design the options and deliver the sessions.

The sessions were self-selected and were not necessarily dependent on age, so children were not hampered by their chronology as they are within the classic school system.

Earlier in the book I talked about education not being the preserve of the teacher and the huge potential of tapping into a community. This is perfectly demonstrated by the university which relied on the community to ensure it had a wide-ranging series of experiences. Many parents have fantastic skills and interests, which due to their own schooling, they don't think can be of value in an educational setting.

Thanks to parents and the wider community, we were able to offer workshops in furniture-making, beauty therapy, hairdressing, cookery, share-dealing, financial management, engineering, painting, languages, cheerleading, contemporary dance, photography, web design, orient-eering, folk music, cricket, gymnastics . . . the list goes on. It was supplemented by workshops led by staff in areas of their own personal interest. Imagine the power of the learning environment where pupils interested enough to select an option are working with adults passionate about that option?

Learning new skills from the pool of parental experience

Because of the number of options available the group sizes varied, but tended to be smaller than the average class, so children got a great opportunity to work and develop their interest. As a school we carefully monitored their progress in workshop options in order to identify new talents, interests or gifts which could be used as the key to maximize each child's potential.

In many ways the university is the element of Grange's development that I was proudest of. As I walked around the school on the first Friday of its implementation, I cried; the dynamic learning and levels of engagement were extraordinary. Staff and children alike had found a new love of school and we had truly created a learning environment that was about expanding minds not simply conditioning them. Children of all academic levels were exploring and discovering new interests, new talents and new ambitions. Having read Ken Robinson's book, I realize that what we had achieved was an environment that gave every one of our pupils the opportunity to be in 'their element'.

We need all kinds of people, successfully filling all kinds of roles, for society to thrive. We need to nurture our future doctors, beauticians, lawyers and bin men; without them we would all be worse off. Like pieces of a jigsaw, each is equally as important for the whole picture. When you sit down with the jigsaw pieces and a box, you don't throw some pieces away because they don't look as interesting; after all a piece that alone resembles a pink blob could turn out to be the *Mona Lisa*'s enigmatic smile.

School is a one-time opportunity. It's job is to help each individual develop and evolve. To find success and fulfilment in their own life, children must be given the options that inhabit the world around them, not just the system they are working in. To truly explore the future of our system and change it for the better, we must look closer at the world we live in and draw on its diversity. We endeavoured to do that at Grange, our vision was captured in three words: LIVING, LEARNING and LAUGHING. Surely this is equally relevant to success in life? As a result of our approach, I can look back with pride on a school filled with all three. Our children and community will grasp the twenty-first century by the neck and make it theirs. We must all do the same if education is to succeed.

CHAPTER 18

Into the unknown

Moving forward from the book

If our children do not look back on their years of schooling with affection, pride and positivity we have failed them!

Author

Sometimes I would walk around my school and watch the children learning, interacting and growing. I often wondered what would become of them. Who would they be? What would their lives hold? What part would our school have played in their success or failure?

I often talk to trainee teachers about the privilege of the profession. Teaching is not just a job, it can't be. We are responsible for the future; not just ours, but the thousands of lives we will touch in our roles. 'To teach is to touch a life forever'. Education is everything. Children spend the majority of their waking lives in school. If we don't get it right, there is no second chance.

Sometimes I would walk around my school when the learning was over and the school was closed. The children's spirit still spilled out onto the corridors and their enthusiasm lit up the empty rooms. Children have a passion and desire for life that burns more powerfully than a flame. Their hopes and aspirations are unclouded by experience and the fear of reality or the unknown. Our children live for today and dream of tomorrow.

Do we really want them to grow to become us? I want my children to grow, to feel confident in the world around them, to feel that they have a sense of purpose, of global belonging. I want my children to have control over their lives; to have the confidence, belief and skills to feel in control of their own destiny.

Carpe diem, seize the day, a phrase originally written by Roman poet Horace, is a salient and thought-provoking challenge to us all. Do we seize the day and, if not, why not?

We live in a world where the majority of us move through life with a sense of powerlessness, a powerlessness that is developed through our childhoods. As children we are taught to do as we are told. We are told that we must because the adults around us know best. This is, of course, the basis of traditional education. Interestingly for me, some of my most powerful learning experiences have come when children in my classes found their own, alternative strategies to problems I thought I had the solutions for and they were teaching me new pathways.

The feeling of powerlessness in education continues throughout our adult lives, most notably when the time comes for us to entrust our most precious things, our children, to the system. Yes, there is the supposed choice of institutions available to us but, no matter where the school or what the reputation, we still leave our kids at the gate and hope.

For many of us, our child's first day is one of the most traumatic of our lives; I have felt it as a parent and seen it as a teacher. We must put our faith in others.

You start to run questions over in your own mind. Will they care for my child the way I do? Will they share my aspirations and dreams. Will my child thrive here? Will he or she be happy?

The vast majority of teachers I have met are passionate about their jobs and the children they work with. The truth, however, is that teachers often feel as powerless as parents to do what they know is right. The increasing politicization of the education system has led to a vastly different agenda. An agenda which is sending our children into a world that is evolving away at speeds that have left the establishment behind. Politicians live in a world dominated by short terms of office, sound bites, media control and performance indicators. They are judged by statistics because none are around long enough to be held to account by real outcome. A child starting school today will more than likely be in the system for a minimum of 13–14 years. Very few governments get that much time to exhibit success. The governments, whoever and wherever they are, do not have that much time, so they need to create instant measurable accountability. They live in a world of self-created targets and statistics, a world that is held to account by figures.

Investment and policy are driven to meet the expectations of these outcomes and altered to respond to the conclusions to make maximum short-term impact.

Their world is perversely controlled by the communication systems of the twenty-first century, by the instant, on-demand generation.

The governments, who represent us, will tell us that the performance culture of statistics and tables is the world that we demanded. They tell us that they were created to make them more accountable to us, to help us understand and set the agenda. They will tell us that they have led to a rapid rise in standards. How do they know? Because their statistics tell us. In education I am regularly told that league tables and high-stakes testing exist because the electorate demands them. Interestingly, I have met very few parents who think high-stakes testing at primary/elementary school age is a good thing. Indeed, behind closed doors, many senior policy makers will agree.

Ownership and empowerment are the keys to education and the transformation our system needs. I do not want my two children to be seen as statistics, ever! My children are human beings, they are unique and I want a system that recognizes that. I want to be able to guarantee that my child leaves school equipped to meet the extraordinary challenges of their future. A 'sorry' from the system that got it wrong, will not be acceptable. Besides, in 20 years, who will still be around to hold to account?

Education is about the future not about the past, yet that is where we find ourselves. Education is politically dangerous because it so emotive. Politicians cannot afford danger, so political safety must come first. As a result, we have created generations of people who are a product of that conservative philosophy. The future is a risky place, it is unknown and it is uncontrollable. The birth of the internet is testament to this. As the first adult generations of the twenty-first century, the future is even scarier because our education did not prepare us to deal with change, with the concept of the unknown. The traditional system deals with certainties, set outcomes, one experience for all. We look to the past to find comfort and reassurance. We cling to the present in the hope that we can stop the revolution into the future. Our leaders rely on our own discomfort in order to justify their own limited aspirations for our tomorrows.

The world hierarchy is changing and the power lies in the hands of the people who are equipping their generations for the future. The new pioneers are not coming from within the established world order and, no matter what we say and how we feel, it is time for us to learn new lessons and reinvent our education systems. It is all very well the policy makers celebrating our past and educational heritage, the fact that we are often held up as the founders of the modern education model. There was a time when we were the centre of the Industrial Revolution. Where did standing still get us then?

While we obsess with basic, traditional educational values the world around us is developing new models that will soon see our children as third world learners. The government in the UK is playing lip service to the challenge, by sanctioning endless research into the future models of curriculum and schooling, but none of it has impacted on the holistic system transformation we need. We have the expertise, the knowledge, the research; sadly, there is not the mainstream political will. Ironically the government in the modern age is too scared to depart from the traditional line.

In some way the system itself is imploding on its own obsession with public opinion. Governments have developed statistical accountability measures and believe that the public will not allow them to look for new approaches. As a result, the system is being driven by statistics, not quality, and our leaders have become stifled by the same thing our education system is doing to our children; strangled by an inability to engage in innovation and change due to the fear of risk.

And this is where we come in. Despite what we may believe, as teachers and as parents, we hold the key. We cannot allow the system to control our children's futures, to hamper their chances, to limit their progress.

As communities we have more opportunity than ever before to take active roles in our children's education. Schools serve their communities and should be accountable to them.

We must not be satisfied by the system or made to feel inadequate by it. Never lose sight of your children and their importance.

Ensure our children's voices are heard. Ask them what they would like for their education to be better. They are experts in the idea of the world of tomorrow. I heard a great question recently, asked of a group of adults, 'Who taught you to text?'

Speak to business leaders in your community and invite them to work together with your school to develop experiences that will help equip children with the skills they need for the future. Forward-thinking organizations know that the earlier they invest in the youth in their local community, the more impact they can have on their future employee base.

Above all, communication holds the key to educational success. We must not be intimidated by developing working partnerships that mould our schools. The truth is that there is far more freedom for schools than many believe. There are schools like Grange, more innovative than Grange, developing the most extraordinary learning experiences for their children which is leading to significant success for the pupils, the staff, the schools and their whole communities. The new blueprints for the future curriculum encourage schools to develop their own, by working with their community to create tailor-made journeys for their children. Get involved and use this book to stimulate discussion.

I have included the examples from Grange to underline that change is possible. We evolved innovative and exciting practices and experiences within the law and within the statutory requirements of the National Curriculum. The results have been extraordinary. I know that our pupils were fit for their futures and will thrive within them. It took courage and a determination to do what was right for our children, not necessarily what was comfortable for us. Our story was written by us all – staff, pupils and the wider community – working together to achieve something of which we were all proud. It was summed up for me when one of our 8-year-old children wrote of Grange, 'I love my school, my school is fantastic and I helped make it great.'

There is a damaging misconception in a number of schools that the Curriculum is restrictive and prevents innovation and change. This is not the case. A few years ago the Department of Education gave schools the opportunity to apply for permission to suspend the National Curriculum if they had rigorous plans to create alternate approaches that would have measurable impact on the pupils. It was called the 'power to innovate'. The Innovation Unit was set up to administer the requests and grant the permissions. In over 90 per cent of the applications and plans submitted the power to innovate was unnecessary, as the schools' proposals were possible within existing legislation.

Schools need the confidence of knowing they have the support of their parents to move forward, to develop for the real benefit of its pupils. I meet so many incredible school leaders who have fantastic plans for their schools, highly innovative plans and forward thinking strategies to drive their schools into the twenty-first century, yet so many of them tell me that they have suppressed those plans because they fear the reaction of their governing body, their parent community, Ofsted, the local authority. They know that their plans will impact on their children, your children, but the barriers that surround them prevent them from making the changes that matter, to the people that matter most.

If, as educators and parents, we work together we can change the system and, when we do, we will be able to look with pride at our grown children and smile when they talk of the chances and dreams they have achieved as a result of their learning.

In a memorable quote, the founder of the Eden Project, Tim Smit says of teachers:

> If all we did was to commit ourselves to leaving this world a better place than we found it, of leading our lives so at the end we could say, 'I am glad I did' rather than 'I wish I had', we would have a chance of creating a beautiful civilisation. In my view, teachers are the lodestone of society. We entrust our most valuable gift, our children and ourselves, to them. If that is so, by definition teachers are the shapers of the future, the architects of a better world by lighting the fires of the imagination and the gentleness of a shared humanity.'
>
> *(T. Smit*, Eden)

To an extent he is right. Teaching is an extraordinary profession, a vocation and, above all, a great privilege. However, teachers cannot educate our children by themselves. It is not teachers or parents who are the shapers of the future it is our children. We can provide them with the materials, the skills and competencies, then it is over to them.

Together, we can prepare our children for their future. If we stand still and do nothing we will have only ourselves to blame. We must not allow ghosts of the past to haunt our children in their future. Together, as parents and educators, we must build a system that will illuminate their world. We must ensure a system that develops in them the skills and experiences to feel confident in their tomorrow. It is up to us not to fear, but to prepare them to lead us into the unknown.

AFTERWORD

Leading into the unknown

In all that I do and all that I say, I will not look back on my life and judge its success by the academic achievements, or otherwise, of my younger days. I want to be able to say that I lived my life and challenged myself, that I gave it my all; created new things and made my mark; that, in my own way, I worked for others. To know that I loved, laughed and was trusted.

I want to know that even as a speck of humanity, I was able to be someone; for myself and others. Of my education all I ask is that you help prepare me to live my dreams.

Author

As we approach the end of the first decade of the twenty-first century we are in the grip of global transformations that have resulted in a new kind of world view. As a species, we now realize that we need to behave and act dramatically differently from our predecessors if we are to bestow upon our future generations any kind of meaningful inheritance. We are a world restricted by fear and a growing awareness of our inability to deal with the changes and challenges ahead.

In many ways, education is a microcosm of that global portrait. We all know things aren't working and in different ways different factions are looking in different directions in the hope of finding solutions. All too often we will resort to the tried and tested, the ways that worked before. Yet what has defined humanity since the dawn of time has been its ability to create, to evolve its thinking, its actions and customs, to invent the world we now inhabit. I remember many years ago striking up a conversation with a retired family friend. He asked me about my dreams and ambitions. I was 8 or 9 at the time and what I wanted was a big house with a pool, a Ferrari and a place in the England soccer team. He turned to me with the sort of smile only wise old family friends can muster and said, with a clarity that still affects me these years later, 'Richard, in my experience, the more you have, the more you want and, most importantly, the more you have will increase the pressure and fear you will live your life under because you will have more to lose.'

I still want the Ferrari and the house with a pool . . . the England dream died on a school playing field when I was trodden into the mud for the third time on a particularly wet November day, but I do understand what he meant. I am not sure that I agree that you should limit your aspirations in order to live a trouble-free life, however, I can recognize in my own life how, at times, I have erred on the side of caution to protect what I have. I also realize, however, that if I don't keep exploring, keep asking what if and taking chances, I will never evolve.

I fear that as we, as a species, have developed, we have gone through the phases of hunger and thirst for new things and now find ourselves so laden with possessions that we can't go further for losing everything. Risk and the ability to take risks are the lifeblood of our evolution and intellect. We cannot afford to sit still, to hunker down and hope that our own inventions and evolution leaves us alone and lets us return to a safer, more rosy-tinted past place.

I believe that education is perhaps more guilty than most at trying to stick for fear of going bust. I believe that at policy level we would rather return to the certainties of the past than explore the possibilities of the future and hope that all the change around us can be contained by the call for 'traditional' values.

Change is a part of everyday life and we are all the better for it. In some ways the world is coming out of great swathes of crisis and our children are hungrier than ever for evolution, for ownership and for new journeys. I truly believe the American decision to elect Barack Obama signalled the intent of a new generation. As a profession and public service, all of us in education need not only to recognize this but to help to develop it and to do that we must start with the way our schools are designed and function.

Of course rhetoric is easy. The practical application, as with so many things, is far, far harder. We are currently an ageing profession that is experiencing a decline in morale and interest in our fold. Teachers span nearly three generations and have varying appetites for the challenges that face us. School leadership is no longer an aspiration for most and for many is seen as a position of management, not one of vision and exploration.

To ensure that we can begin the process of transformation, not reform, that is the imperative; we must do a number of things:

First, we must come to terms with the fact that change is part of education and will always be so. It is not a job for conservatives who want the same thing day after day, year after year. I've planned it and resourced it so now I'm going to teach it until my pension clicks in! Schools of today and certainly of tomorrow must be dynamic entities, constantly innovating and driving change; cultures of risk-taking, creativity and development. For that to be the case, we need to attract the right kind of people to work in our schools and then nurture the right ones to lead them. Education is not the career of choice for most of our young people because it is just not cool . . . but it should be.

Secondly, we must stimulate and build the momentum for change by developing cultures that constantly question and explore what is happening and what could happen. Grange's phenomenal development occurred because of the culture that promoted constant discussion, questioning and action. We had no completed, timescaled or costed action plans and definite outcomes at the start of our journey. We committed to asking ourselves questions and finding ways to answer them; 'How do we create Disneyland?' To ensure progress and real development there must be a move away from the culture that so many of us live by where things end with a 'Yeah, but'. We need to develop cultures where problems are seen as challenges, as opportunities for creativity.

Thirdly, we must develop a tangible sense of empowerment and regain the feeling that teaching is a profession. A profession that contains talented people, of significant value and vision, who truly are drawn to the vocation because of their desire to give all of our children the best start to life. We must realize that teachers and those directly involved with our children do know best and are the ones who really do have our children's best interests at heart; not the media, the civil servants in government offices or the politicians. In a time of change and a time where we have an unprecedented level of control over our own lives, we must use it all to take control of education and its development for our children.

As I finish this book I confess what I am sure those of you who have made it to the end with me will already know: I am not a great academic or intellectual. I admire those who are; those who use those gifts for the good, anyway, but I do feel that our future lies not in the few who know or think that they know. It lies in those who are confident enough to realize that they don't; those who then have the courage, resilience and creativity to find out. In essence, this is where the journey in our schools must begin. We must build a culture that recognizes that learning, great learning, just opens doors to new learning and to greater questions. The school of the future recognizes that the future will always be unknown but that, by learning to deal with it, live within in it and be excited by it, we will provide our children with the education they will need and that they deserve.

Richard Gerver, 2009

Bibliography and references

Burke, C. and Grosvenor, I. (2003), *The School I'd Like*. London: RoutledgeFalmer.

Carnegie, D. (1939), *How to Win Friends and Influence People*. New York: Simon & Schuster.

Chartered Institute of Educational Assessors (7 December 2008), 'Exams: The Sweet Smell of Success or that Sinking Feeling?'. Press release.

Claxton, G. (2002), *Building Learning Power*. Bristol: TLO Ltd.

Cohen, A. K. (1955), *Delinquent Boys: The Culture of the Gang*. Glencoe: The Free Press.

Devlin, M. (2006). 'Inequality and the Stereotyping of Young People'. Report for The National Youth Council of Ireland and The Equality Authority. Dublin: The Equality Authority.

Faculty of Arts and Science, University of Toronto (2006). 'LOL, where r u?: Teen Talk in Instant Messaging'. *Ideas: The Arts and Science Review*, vol. 3. no. 2.

Fletcher, K. M. (2002). 'Guidelines for Knowledge Management from the Phenomenological Literature'. Pac Rim Cross Consulting.

Gardner, H. (1983), *Frames of Mind: The Theory of Multiple Intelligences*. New York: Basic Books.

Gilbert. D. T. (2003), *The Selected Works of Edward E. Jones*. New Jersey: John Wiley & Sons.

Gottfried, J., Smith, A., Rugg, M. and Dolan, R. (2004), 'Remembrance of Odors Past: Human Olfractory Cortex in Cross-Modal Recognition Memory'. *Neuron*, vol. 42, 4.

Gratton, L. (2007), *Hot Spots*. Upper Saddle River: Prentice Hall.

Gross, K. (2006), 'Effects of Year 12 Stress on Mental Health'. *Youth Studies Australia*. Australian Clearing House for Youth Studies: University of Tasmania.

Her Majesty's Government (2004), 'Every Child Matters: Change for Children'. DFES-1109-2004.

Hirsh, D. (2009), *Ending Child Poverty in a Changing Economy*. York: Joseph Rowntree Foundation.

Institute for Public Policy (10 December 2007), 'Asbo Culture: Making Kids Criminal'. Press release.

Johnson, S. (2005), *Everything Bad is Good for You*. London: Penguin Books.

Kreitzman, L. and Foster, R. (2004), *The Rhythms of Life: The Biological Clocks that Control the Daily Lives of Every Living Thing*. London: Profile Books.

National Advisory Committee on Creative and Cultural Education (1999), 'All Our Futures: Creativity, Culture and Education'. Report to the Secretaries of State for Education, Employment and Culture, Media and Sport.

The National Children's Bureau (2009). 'Media Portrayal of Young People'.

OECD (2006), *Schooling for Tomorrow: Personalising Education*. Paris: OECD Publishing.

Phi Delta Kappa International (2009), 'Americans Speak Out: Are Educators and Policy Makers Listening? The 41st Phi Delta Kappa/Gallop Poll of the Public Attitudes Towards the Public Schools'. Indiana: Phi Delta Kappa International Inc.

Plester, B., Wood, C. and Joshi, P. (2009). 'Exploring the Relationship between Children's Knowledge of Text Message Abbreviations and Social Literacy Outcomes'. *British Journal of Developmental Psychology*, vol. 27, no. 1.

Prensky, M. (2001) 'Digital Natives, Digital Immigrants'. *On the Horizon*, vol. 9, no. 5. Washington: MCB University Press.

Rasmussen, J. (1983), 'Skills, rules, knowledge: signals, signs, and symbols, and other distinctions in human performance models'. *IEEE Transactions on Systems, Man and Cybernetics*, 13, 257–266.

Roberts, K. (2005), *Lovemarks: The Future beyond Brands*. Brooklyn: Powerhouse Books.

Robinson, K. (2001), *Out of Our Minds: Learning to be Creative*. Oxford: Capstone Publishing Ltd.

Robinson, K. (2009), *The Element: How Finding Your Passion Changes Everything*. New York: Penguin Books.

Rose, J. (2009), 'Independent Review of Primary Curriculum: Final Report'. Department for Children, Schools and Family. DCSF-00499-2009.

Sale, Jonathan (19 March 2009), 'Passed/Failed: the Life of Duncan Bannetyne, Entrepreneur and Dragon's Den Panellist'. *The Independent*.

Scase, R. (2007). *Global Remix: The Fight for Competitive Advantage*. London: Kogan Page.

Smit, T. (2001) *Eden*. London: Bantam Press.

Smith, A. (2002), *The Brain's Behind It: New Knowledge about the Brain and Learning*. Stafford: Network Educational Press.

Taggart, C. (2008), *I Used to Know That*. London: Michael O'Mara Books Ltd.

Teese, R., Charlton, M. and Polesel, J. (1997), 'Queensland State High School Students: Participation, Achievement, Attitudes and Post-schooling Plans'. Report for the Queensland Department of Education Educational Outcomes Research Unit. Melbourne: University of Melbourne.

Welsh, J. (2001), *Straight From the Gut*. New York: Time Warner Books.

Woodhead, C. (2002), *Class War*. New York: Time Warner Books.

Useful websites

All Our Futures, www.culture.gov.uk/naccce.PDF
Apple, www.apple.com
Bannatyne, Duncan, www.bannatyne.co.uk
Caan, James, www.james-caan.com
Calouste Gulbenkian Foundation, www.gulbenkian.org.uk
Chartered Institute of Educational Assessors, www.ciea.org.uk
Claxton, Guy, www.guyclaxton.com
Demos, www.demos.co.uk
Department for Children, Schools and Families, www.dcsf.gov.uk
Diploma, www.direct.gov.uk/diplomas
Eden Project, www.edenproject.com
EGG, www.egg.com
Futurelab, www.futurelab.org.uk; www.futurelab.org.uk/projects/teaching-with-games
Gardner, Howard, www.howardgardner.com
Grange Primary School, www.grangeton.com
Harley Davidson, www.harley-davidson.com
Heppell, Stephen, www.heppell.net
Innovation Unit, www.innovation-unit.co.uk
Institute for Public Policy, www.ippr.org
Jones, John, www.sirjohnjones.com
Joseph Roundtree Foundation, www.jrf.org.uk
Lawn Tennis Association, www.lta.org.uk
Microsoft, www.microsoft.com
Monkseaton High School, www.monkseaton.org.uk
Mud Valley, www.mudvalley.co.uk
Nike, www.nike.com
Not School, www.inclusiontrust.org/notschool
Office for Standards in Education, www.ofsted.gov.uk
Prensky, Marc, www.marcprensky.com/writing
Pixar, www.pixar.com
Popular Mechanics, www.popularmechanics.com
Primary Curriculum Review, www.dcsf.gov.uk/primarycurriculumreview
Programme for International Student Assessment (PISA), www.pisa.oecd.org
Qualifications and Curriculum Authority, www.qca.org.uk
Robinson, Ken, www.sirkenrobinson.com
RSA, www.thersa.org
Second Life, www.secondlife.com
The Sims (EA Games), www.thesims.ea.com
SLIC Best Practices in Teaching, www.slbestpractices2007.wikispaces.com
Smith, Alistair, www.alite.co.uk
Somerset County Council,
    www.six.somerset.gov.uk/sixv3/do_download.asp?did=16781

Index